HOUGHTON MIFFLIN HARCOURT

# SOCIAL STUDIES

## NEW YORK CITY

## WORLD COMMUNITIES
## NOW AND LONG AGO

### Program Authors

Dr. Herman J. Viola
Dr. Sarah Witham Bednarz
Dr. Carlos E. Cortés

Dr. Cheryl Jennings
Dr. Mark C. Schug
Dr. Charles S. White

Visit  Education Place®
www.eduplace.com/kids

HOUGHTON MIFFLIN HARCOURT

## Authors

**Senior Author**
**Dr. Herman J. Viola**
Curator Emeritus
Smithsonian Institution

**Dr. Cheryl Jennings**
**Project Director**
Florida Institute of Education
University of North Florida

**Dr. Sarah Witham Bednarz**
**Associate Professor, Geography**
Texas A&M University

**Dr. Mark C. Schug**
**Professor and Director**
Center for Economic Education
University of Wisconsin, Milwaukee

**Dr. Carlos E. Cortés**
**Professor Emeritus, History**
University of California, Riverside

**Dr. Charles S. White**
**Associate Professor**
School of Education
Boston University

## Program Consultants

**Philip J. Deloria**
Associate Professor
Department of History and
Program in American Studies
University of Michigan

**Lucien Ellington**
UC Professor of Education and Asia
Program Co-Director
University of Tennessee, Chattanooga

**Thelma Wills Foote**
Associate Professor
University of California

**Stephen J. Fugita**
Distinguished Professor
Psychology and Ethnic Studies
Santa Clara University

**Charles C. Haynes**
Senior Scholar
First Amendment Center

**Ted Hemmingway**
Professor of History
The Florida Agricultural &
Mechanical University

**Douglas Monroy**
Professor of History
The Colorado College

**Lynette K. Oshima**
Assistant Professor
Department of Language, Literacy
and Sociocultural Studies and Social
Studies Program Coordinator
University of New Mexico

**Jeffrey Strickland**
Assistant Professor, History
University of Texas Pan American

**Clifford E. Trafzer**
Professor of History and
American Indian Studies
University of California

Printed in the U.S.A.

ISBN: 978-0-547-19758-6     0-547-19758-6

23456789-0868- 17 16 15 14 13 12 11 10

# New York State Social Studies Standards
## Elementary School

## STANDARD 1

### HISTORY OF THE UNITED STATES AND NEW YORK

**Students will use a variety of intellectual skills to demonstrate their understanding of major ideas, eras, themes, developments, and turning points in the history of the United States and New York.**

1.1 The study of New York State and United States history requires an analysis of the development of American culture, its diversity and multicultural context, and the ways people are unified by many values, practices, and traditions.

1.2 Important ideas, social and cultural values, beliefs, and traditions from New York State and United States history illustrate the connections and interactions of people and events across time and from a variety of perspectives.

1.3 The study about the major social, political, economic, cultural, and religious developments in New York State and United States history involves learning about the important roles and contributions of individuals and groups.

1.4 The skills of historical analysis include the ability to: explain the significance of historical evidence, weigh the importance, reliability, and validity of evidence, understand the concept of multiple causation, and understand the importance of changing and competing interpretations of different historical developments.

## STANDARD 2

### WORLD HISTORY

**Students will use a variety of intellectual skills to demonstrate their understanding of major ideas, eras, themes, developments, and turning points in world history and examine the broad sweep of history from a variety of perspectives.**

2.1 The study of world history requires an understanding of world cultures and civilizations, including an analysis of important ideas, social and cultural values, beliefs, and traditions. This study also examines the human condition and the connections and interactions of people across time and space and the ways different people view the same event or issue from a variety of perspectives.

2.2 Establishing timeframes, exploring different periodizations, examining themes across time and within cultures, and focusing on important turning points in world history help organize the study of world cultures and civilizations.

2.3 The study of the major social, political, cultural, and religious developments in world history involves learning about the important roles and contributions of individuals and groups.

2.4 The skills of historical analysis include the ability to investigate differing and competing interpretations of the theories of history, hypothesize about why interpretations change over time, explain the importance of historical evidence, and understand the concepts of change and continuity over time.

**iii**

## STANDARD 3

### GEOGRAPHY

**Students will use a variety of intellectual skills to demonstrate their understanding of the geography of the interdependent world in which we live — local, national, and global — including the distribution of people, places, and environments over the Earth's surface.**

3.1 Geography can be divided into six essential elements, which can be used to analyze important historic, geographic, economic, and environmental questions and issues. These six elements include: the world in spatial terms, places and regions, physical settings (including natural resources), human systems, environment and society, and the use of geography.

3.2 Geography requires the development and application of the skills of asking and answering geography questions, analyzing theories of geography, and acquiring and organizing geographic information.

## STANDARD 4

### ECONOMICS

**Students will use a variety of intellectual skills to demonstrate their understanding of how the United States and other societies develop economic systems and associated institutions to allocate scarce resources, how major decision-making units function in the U.S. and other national economies, and how an economy solves the scarcity problem through market and non-market mechanisms.**

4.1 The study of economics requires an understanding of major economic concepts and systems, the principles of economic decision making, and the interdependence of economies and economic systems throughout the world.

4.2 Economics requires the development and application of the skills needed to make informed and well-reasoned economic decisions in daily and national life.

## STANDARD 5

### CIVICS, CITIZENSHIP, AND GOVERNMENT

**Students will use a variety of intellectual skills to demonstrate their understanding of the necessity for establishing governments, the governmental system of the United States and other nations, the United States Constitution, the basic civic values of American constitutional democracy, and the roles, rights, and responsibilities of citizenship, including avenues of participation.**

5.1 The study of civics, citizenship, and government involves learning about political systems; the purposes of government and civic life; and the differing assumptions held by people across time and place regarding power, authority, governance, and law.

5.2 The state and federal governments established by the Constitutions of the United States and the State of New York embody basic civic values (such as justice, honesty, self-discipline, due process, equality, majority rule with respect for minority rights, and respect for self, others, and property), principles, and practices and establish a system of shared and limited government.

5.3 Central to civics and citizenship is an understanding of the roles of the citizen within American constitutional democracy and the scope of a citizen's rights and responsibilities.

5.4 The study of civics and citizenship requires the ability to probe ideas and assumptions, ask and answer analytical questions, take a skeptical attitude toward questionable arguments, evaluate evidence, formulate rational conclusions, and develop and refine participatory skills.

# World Geography and Culture

1

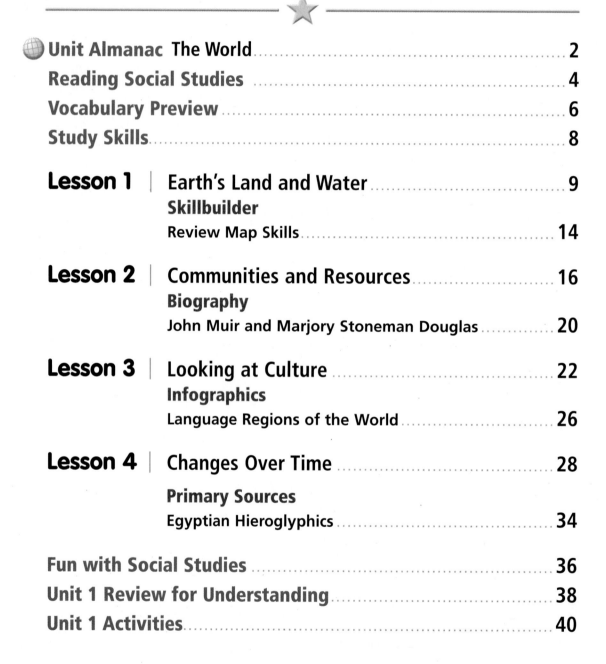

🌐 **Unit Almanac** The World ........................................ 2

**Reading Social Studies** ............................................ 4

**Vocabulary Preview** ............................................... 6

**Study Skills** ...................................................... 8

**Lesson 1** | Earth's Land and Water ............................. 9
**Skillbuilder**
Review Map Skills ................................................ 14

**Lesson 2** | Communities and Resources ..................... 16
**Biography**
John Muir and Marjory Stoneman Douglas ............... 20

**Lesson 3** | Looking at Culture ............................... 22
**Infographics**
Language Regions of the World ............................. 26

**Lesson 4** | Changes Over Time ............................... 28
**Primary Sources**
Egyptian Hieroglyphics ....................................... 34

**Fun with Social Studies** ....................................... 36
**Unit 1 Review for Understanding** ........................... 38
**Unit 1 Activities** ................................................ 40

NYC UNIT 2

# Africa

Unit Almanac Africa Today ........................... 42

Reading Social Studies ........................... 44

Vocabulary Preview ........................... 46

Study Skills ........................... 48

**Lesson 1** | This Is Africa ........................... 49
Skillbuilder
Read a Map Scale ........................... 54

**Lesson 2** | Case Study
Nigeria: Land and Economy ........................... 56
Infographics
Nigeria's Oil ........................... 62

Skillbuilder
Read a History Timeline ........................... 64

**Lesson 3** | Case Study
Nigeria: History and Government ........................... 66
Primary Sources
Royal Art of Benin ........................... 72

**Lesson 4** | Case Study
Nigeria: People and Culture ........................... 74
Celebrate Nigeria ........................... 80

Biography
Wole Soyinka ........................... 82

Fun with Social Studies ........................... 84

Unit 2 Review for Understanding ........................... 86

Unit 2 Activities ........................... 88

🌐 **Unit Almanac** Asia Today ........................................ **90**

**Reading Social Studies** ............................................. **92**

**Vocabulary Preview** ................................................ **94**

**Study Skills** ........................................................ **96**

**Lesson 1** | This Is Asia .......................................... **97**
Skillbuilder
Read a Bar Graph ..................................................... **102**

**Lesson 2** | Case Study
China: Land and Economy ............................................ **104**
Infographics
Made in China ........................................................ **110**

**Lesson 3** | Case Study
China: History and Government ..................................... **112**
Biography
Women Leaders ...................................................... **118**

Skillbuilder
Identify Primary and Secondary Sources ........................... **120**

**Lesson 4** | Case Study
China: People and Culture .......................................... **122**
Celebrate China ...................................................... **128**

Primary Sources
Sayings of Confucius ................................................. **130**

**Fun with Social Studies** .......................................... **132**

**Unit 3 Review for Understanding** ............................... **134**

**Unit 3 Activities** .................................................. **136**

# NYC UNIT 4 Europe

**137**

🌐 **Unit Almanac Europe Today** .................................................. 138

**Reading Social Studies** ........................................................... 140

**Vocabulary Preview** ................................................................ 142

**Study Skills** ............................................................................ 144

**Lesson 1** | **This Is Europe** ................................................... 145
Skillbuilder
Choose the Right Source ........................................................... 150

**Lesson 2** | Case Study
**Italy: Land and Economy** ...................................................... 152
Primary Sources
Venice's Grand Canal ................................................................. 158

**Lesson 3** | Case Study
**Italy: History and Government** ............................................. 160
Infographics
A Roman House .......................................................................... 166

Skillbuilder
Resolve Conflicts ........................................................................ 168

**Lesson 4** | Case Study
**Italy: People and Culture** ...................................................... 170
Celebrate Italy ........................................................................... 176

Biography
Italian Athletes .......................................................................... 178

**Fun with Social Studies** ......................................................... 180

**Unit 4 Review for Understanding** ......................................... 182

**Unit 4 Activities** ..................................................................... 184

# South America

🌐 **Unit Almanac** South America Today .......................... 186

**Reading Social Studies** ........................................ 188

**Vocabulary Preview** ........................................... 190

**Study Skills** ................................................... 192

**Lesson 1** | This Is South America ............................ 193
Skillbuilder
Use Latitude and Longitude ..................................... 198

**Lesson 2** | Case Study
Brazil: Land and Economy ....................................... 200
Infographics
Hi-Tech Brazil ................................................... 206

**Lesson 3** | Case Study
Brazil: History and Government ................................. 208
Primary Sources
Visiting the Amazon Rain Forest ................................ 214
Skillbuilder
Point of View ................................................... 216

**Lesson 4** | Case Study
Brazil: People and Culture ..................................... 218
Celebrate Brazil ................................................ 224
Biography
Marina Silva .................................................... 226

**Fun with Social Studies** ..................................... 228

**Unit 5 Review for Understanding** ............................. 230

**Unit 5 Activities** ............................................ 232

# Resources

Five Themes of Geography .......... R2

Atlas ............................. R4

Glossary .......................... R24

Index ............................. R29

Acknowledgments ................... R36

# Features

## Biography

Protecting Resources                     20
   John Muir
   Marjory Stoneman Douglas
Wole Soyinka                             82
Women Leaders                            118
   Fu Hao
   Empress Lü
Italian Athletes                         178
   Fabio Cannavaro
   Andrea Bargnani
   Stefania Belmondo
Marina Silva                             226

## Infographics

Language Regions of the World            26
Nigeria's Oil                            62
Made in China                            110
A Roman House                            166
Hi-Tech Brazil                           206

## Primary Sources

Egyptian Hieroglyphics                   34
Royal Art of Benin                       72
Sayings of Confucius                     130
Venice's Grand Canal                     158
Visiting the Amazon Rain Forest          214

# Skill Lessons

Take a step-by-step approach to learning and practicing key social studies skills.

## Reading Social Studies

| | |
|---|---|
| Main Idea and Details | 4 |
| Compare and Contrast | 44 |
| Summarize | 92 |
| Generalize | 140 |
| Cause and Effect | 188 |

## Unit Study Skills

| | |
|---|---|
| Preview and Question | 8 |
| Make an Outline | 48 |
| Use a K-W-L Chart | 96 |
| Use an Anticipation Guide | 144 |
| Write to Learn | 192 |

## Map and Globe Skills

| | |
|---|---|
| Review Map Skills | 14 |
| Read a Map Scale | 54 |
| Use Latitude and Longitude | 198 |

Skill Practice: Reading Maps
**51, 57, 58, 67, 105, 153, 161, 195, 201, 202**

## Chart and Graph Skills

| | |
|---|---|
| Read a History Timeline | 64 |
| Read a Bar Graph | 102 |

Skill Practice: Reading Charts
**24, 70, 116**

Skill Practice: Reading Graphs
**75, 135**

Skill Practice: Reading Timelines
**87, 163, 211**

## Study Skills

| | |
|---|---|
| Identify Primary and Secondary Sources | 120 |
| Choose the Right Source | 150 |

Skill Practice: Reading Visuals
**10, 12, 154**

## Citizenship Skills

| | |
|---|---|
| Resolve Conflicts | 168 |
| Point of View | 216 |

## Reading Skills/Graphic Organizer

Categorize
**16**

Cause and Effect
**56, 193**

Compare and Contrast
**49**

Generalize
**104, 145, 200**

Main Idea and Details
**9, 22, 74, 122, 160, 218**

Problem and Solution
**152**

Sequence
**28, 66, 112, 208**

Summarize
**97, 170**

# Visual Learning

## Maps

| | |
|---|---|
| The World | 2 |
| World Continents | 15 |
| Language Regions of the World | 26 |
| New York | 39 |
| Africa Today | 42 |
| Africa's Landforms | 51 |
| Cities in Africa | 55 |
| Nigeria's Landforms | 57 |
| Jobs in Nigeria | 58 |
| Kingdoms in Early Nigeria | 67 |
| Asia Today | 90 |
| Asia's Landforms | 99 |
| China's Landforms | 105 |
| Jobs in China | 106 |
| Trade Route from China to the United States | 110 |
| Europe Today | 138 |
| Europe's Landforms | 147 |
| Italy's Landforms | 153 |
| Jobs in Italy | 154 |
| Roman Empire | 161 |
| South America Today | 186 |
| South America's Landforms | 195 |
| Latitude Lines | 198 |
| Longitude Lines | 198 |
| The World | 199 |
| Brazil's Landforms | 201 |
| Jobs in Brazil | 202 |
| South America | 231 |
| The World: Political | R4 |
| The World: Physical | R6 |
| United States: Political | R8 |
| United States: Physical | R10 |
| Africa: Political | R12 |
| Africa: Physical | R13 |
| Asia: Political | R14 |
| Asia: Physical | R16 |
| Europe: Political | R18 |
| Europe: Physical | R20 |
| South America: Political | R22 |
| South America: Physical | R23 |

## Charts and Graphs

| | |
|---|---|
| Mountains Around the World | 3 |
| Rivers Around the World | 3 |
| Comparing Cultures | 24 |
| Comparing Languages | 26 |
| African Countries with the Most People | 43 |
| Top Winners of the Africa Cup of Nations | 43 |
| Nigeria's Government | 70 |
| Largest Groups in Nigeria | 75 |
| Asian Countries with the Most People | 91 |
| Asia's Internet Users, 2005 | 91 |
| Asia | 96 |
| Independent Countries of the World | 103 |
| China's Top Export Countries, 2007 | 110 |
| China's Government, Then and Now | 116 |
| Large Cities in China | 135 |
| European Countries with the Most People | 139 |
| Visitors to Europe, 2004 | 139 |
| Italy's Leaders | 165 |
| South American Countries with the Most People | 187 |
| South American Languages | 187 |
| Voting in Brazil and the United States | 212 |
| School Calendar in Brazil | 222 |

## Diagrams and Infographics

| | |
|---|---|
| Geographic Features | 10 |
| Three Kinds of Resources | 17 |
| Language Regions of the World | 26 |
| From Oil to Gasoline | 63 |
| Trade Route from China to the United States | 110 |
| A Roman House | 166 |
| Hi-Tech Brazil | 206 |

## Timelines

| | |
|---|---|
| History Timeline | 65 |
| Nigeria's History | 68 |
| Nigeria Timeline | 87 |
| China's Leaders | 114 |
| Italy's History | 162 |
| Important Dates in Brazil's History | 210 |

# Constitution Day

**The United States Constitution is one of the most important documents of our nation.** It has its own special day on September 17. On this day more than 200 years ago, the document was signed by leaders of the new United States. The Constitution is our country's source for rules and laws. It tells us what the government can and cannot do. It also protects people's rights.

Today, we celebrate Constitution Day and Citizenship Day during the week of September 17. On this day, citizens remember what the Constitution says and why it is important to us.

**Visitors can view the original Constitution at the National Archives Building in Washington, D.C.**

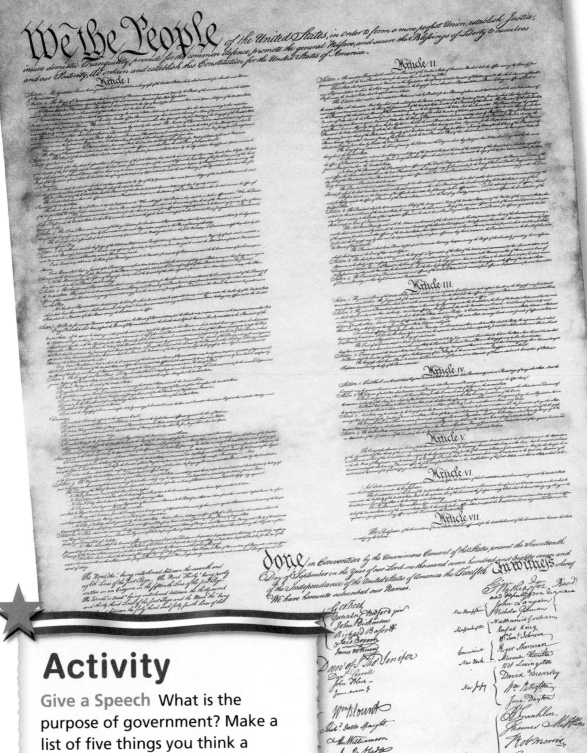

# Activity

**Give a Speech** What is the purpose of government? Make a list of five things you think a government should do. Then choose one thing from your list and prepare a speech that explains why it is important.

# World Geography and Culture

The Unisphere sculpture, Queens, New York

**The Big Idea**

What are the important features of communities throughout the world?

**WHAT TO KNOW**

✓ What are geographic features?

✓ What resources do communities use?

✓ What are some parts of culture?

✓ In what ways have cultures changed over time?

The World

ARCTIC OCEAN

Greenland

▲ Mt. McKinley (Denali)

Iceland

NORTH AMERICA

Baffin Island

ROCKY MOUNTAINS

GREAT BASIN

Great Lakes

Newfoundland

GREAT PLAINS

Missouri River

Mississippi River

APPALACHIAN MTS.

Hawaiian Islands

Colorado R.

Rio Grande

ATLANTIC OCEAN

EUROPE

ALPS

Mediterranean Sea

SAHARA

S A H E L

Nile River

Red Sea

AFRICA

ETHIOPIAN HIGHLAND

Congo River

CONGO BASIN

Lake Victoria

▲ Mt. Kilimanjaro

PACIFIC OCEAN

Gulf of Mexico

Cuba

ATLANTIC OCEAN

Caribbean Sea

CENTRAL AMERICA

Equator

Galápagos Islands

AMAZON

Amazon River

BASIN

BRAZILIAN HIGHLANDS

ANDES MTS.

SOUTH AMERICA

KALAHARI DESERT

Madagas

km 0   500   1,000
mi 0   500   1,000

N
W    E
S

Mt. Aconcagua

### KEY
High mountains
Low mountains
Plains
Coastal plains
Ice cap

Greenland

ARCTIC
OCEAN

Iceland

SIBERIA

Lena R.

URAL MOUNTAINS

Ob River

ASIA

Volga
River

Black Sea

Aral
Sea

ALTAI MTS.

Caspian
Sea

GOBI DESERT

East
Sea

ARABIAN
PENINSULA

PLATEAU
OF TIBET

Chang Jiang
(Yangtze)

HIMALAYA MTS.

Indus River

Mt. Everest

Ganges River

Mekong River

DECCAN
PLATEAU

INDOCHINA
PENINSULA

Red Sea

Arabian
Sea

Bay
of
Bengal

South China Sea

Sri Lanka

Borneo

Equator

Sumatra

gascar

INDIAN
OCEAN

N
W    E
S

GREAT
SANDY
DESERT

AUSTRALIA

km  0    500   1,000
mi  0    500    1,000

## Mountains Around the World

Height (in feet)

30,000

20,000

10,000

0

Everest    Aconcagua    McKinley    Kilimanjaro

Mountain

## Rivers Around the World

River

Nile

Amazon

Chang Jiang

Mississippi

0    1,500    3,000    4,500

Length (in miles)

Think about the mountains and rivers near where you live.

- What is the highest mountain in your state?
- What is the longest river that runs through your state?

# Reading Social Studies

## Main Idea and Details

**Why It Matters** Knowing the main idea helps you better understand what you have read.

## Learn the Skill

The **main idea** is the most important idea of a paragraph or passage. The main idea is often in the first sentence of a passage. **Details** give more information about the main idea.

Main Idea

Detail 1    Detail 2    Detail 3

## Practice the Skill

Read the paragraph below. Find the main idea. Then find the supporting details.

**Main Idea**  The Great Lakes are so big that they have an effect on the weather, known as the lake effect. Tiny drops of lake water **Details**  enter the air. In winter, the wet air is blown toward the east by the wind. Heavy snow then falls on the land there.

# Apply the Skill

Read the paragraphs, and answer the questions.

# The Great Lakes

The Great Lakes are the world's largest group of freshwater lakes. Most of the lakes are located in both the United States and Canada. They begin at the northeastern corner of Minnesota. They end at the northwestern corner of New York.

Lakes Superior, Michigan, and Huron are the largest Great Lakes. At 350 miles long and 160 miles wide, Lake Superior is the largest lake on Earth. East of Lake Superior is Lake Michigan. It is 307 miles long and 118 miles wide. Farther east is Lake Huron, the second-largest Great Lake. It is 206 miles long and up to 183 miles wide.

Lakes Erie and Ontario are the farthest east of the Great Lakes. At 241 miles long and 57 miles wide, Lake Erie is the fourth-largest Great Lake. It flows into Lake Ontario, the smallest Great Lake. Lake Ontario is 193 miles long and up to 53 miles wide.

## Main Idea and Details

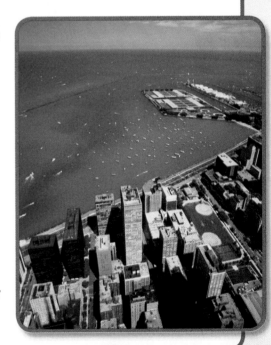

1. What is the main idea of this selection?

2. What are the names of the Great Lakes?

3. Which Great Lake is the largest?

View of Lake Michigan from a Chicago skyscraper

# Vocabulary Preview

## climate

The **climate,** or the weather over a period of time, is different in various parts of the world. Climates may be warm or cold, wet or dry. **page 12**

## natural resources

Water and plants are found in nature. People depend on these **natural resources** to live.

**page 16**

## Reading Strategy

**Question** Use the question strategy for Lessons 1 and 2.

**Monitor and Clarify** Use the monitor and clarify strategy for Lessons 3 and 4.

### ethnic group

People in the United States come from many different cultures and **ethnic groups**.
**page 25**

### government

In the United States, people choose **government** leaders. These leaders make and carry out laws. **page 32**

Go Digital visit www.eduplace.com/nycssp/

# Study Skills

## PREVIEW AND QUESTION

Previewing a lesson helps you identify main ideas. Asking questions about these ideas can help you find important information.

- Reading the lesson title and section titles gives clues about the main topic. Think of any questions you have about the topic.

- Read to find the answers to your questions.

- Finally, review what you have read.

| World Geography and Culture | | | |
|---|---|---|---|
| Preview | Questions | Read | Review |
| **Lesson 1** A landform is a feature of Earth's surface. | What kinds of landforms are there? | ✓ | ✓ |
| **Lesson 2** Natural resources are things found in nature that people use. | | | |

# Earth's Land and Water

▶ **WHAT TO KNOW**
What are geographic features?

▶ **VOCABULARY**

**landform**
**continent**
**geography**
**climate**
**adapt**

**READING SKILL**
**Main Idea and Details**
As you read, list details that tell ways geographic features affect people.

**Before You Read** Have you ever ridden a bike on a hill? Riding down is easy. Going up is harder. You pedal hard going up hills. On a bike, you see how the land slopes up or down.

## Landforms and Continents

The hill that you rode on is a landform. A **landform** is a shape or feature on the Earth's surface. Mountains are landforms that are taller than hills. Plains are low landforms that are flat or gently rolling. Plateaus are also flat, but they are high and sometimes have steep sides.

Landforms are found on every continent on Earth. A **continent** is a large area of land. There are seven continents on Earth. They are Africa, Antarctica, Asia, Australia, Europe, North America, and South America.

*main idea*

**Earth**
This photograph from space shows part of North America.

# Living on Land and Water

When you think about Earth and its continents, you are thinking about geography. **Geography** is the study of people, places, and Earth. Landforms are one part, or feature, of geography. Bodies of water are also geographic features.

Oceans are the largest bodies of water on Earth. They surround the continents. Oceans cover more than two-thirds of Earth. Parts of oceans have names. A sea is a smaller part of an ocean, or a body of salt water surrounded by land. A gulf is a large area of the ocean partly surrounded by land.

Each continent also has smaller bodies of water. Rivers are bodies of water that flow downhill. Lakes are bodies of fresh water surrounded by land.

**Bodies of Water**  Rivers and streams flow downstream to oceans.
**Skill  Reading Visuals**  What landforms are shown?

source of river

stream

hills

lake

river

plains

wetland

bay

## Where People Live

Earth's geographic features affect where people build communities. People often choose to live on plains. The land there is level, or flat, so people can easily farm, build homes, and travel.

Many people also live in valleys. A valley is the land between mountains or hills. The rich soil at the bottom of valleys can be good for farming. Fewer communities are built in the mountains. Mountains can be rugged and have steep slopes. It can be hard to grow crops on high slopes.

Bodies of water also affect where people live. Many cities are built near oceans, rivers, or lakes. People build communities near water so they can have fresh water for drinking and for growing crops. People also live near water because they can travel easily in boats.

✓ **READING CHECK** MAIN IDEA AND DETAILS What geographic features do people choose to live on or near?

mountains

waterfall

valley

gulf

ocean

Lake Baikal, in Russia

The Nile River, in Egypt

Winter weather near Cairns, Australia, (left) and in Bavaria, Germany, (right) are very different.

**Skill** **Reading Visuals** What clues about the climate do you see in each photograph?

## Weather and Climate

What is the weather like today? Is it rainy or windy? Weather is what the air is like at a certain place and time. Weather affects people at work and play. For example, on snowy days, people might stay home until snowplows clear the roads.

Another geographic feature of every place on Earth is climate. **Climate** is the weather of a place over a long period of time. Climates can be warm or cold, wet or dry. They may have seasons. Climates are affected by landforms and water. The cool water in an ocean tends to cool nearby air in the summer. The climate in high mountains is cooler than in low valleys.

## Climate Makes a Difference

People adapt to different climates. To **adapt** is to change to fit a new place or event. People adapt to their climate by choosing shelter and clothing that meet their needs. In a cold climate, people wear coats and hats outdoors. In hot climates, people may cool their homes and businesses year-round.

Climate also affects the plants that grow and the animals that live in an area. Some plants, such as cactus, grow well in areas with little rain. Certain animals, such as some kinds of horned lizards, live only in a hot climate.

✓**READING CHECK** CAUSE AND EFFECT
How do people adapt to a hot climate?

**Horned lizard**

**SUMMARY**

Landforms and bodies of water are some of Earth's geographic features. These features affect how and where people choose to live.

## Lesson Review

**1** **WHAT TO KNOW** What are geographic features?

**2** **VOCABULARY** Write two sentences that tell about the kind of **climate** where you live.

**3** **CRITICAL THINKING: Compare and Contrast** In what ways might living near a river be similar to living on a plain? What would be different?

**4** **WRITING ACTIVITY** Write a paragraph about the landforms or water in your community. Describe how people have adapted to them.

**5** **MAIN IDEA AND DETAILS** Complete the graphic organizer to show how geographic features affect people.

## Skillbuilder

# Review Map Skills

Different kinds of maps show different information. They usually have parts that are the same, though. The parts of a map help you understand the information on the map.

map title

map key

compass rose

cardinal directions

intermediate directions

## Learn the Skill

**Step 1:** Read the map title, or name of the map. The **map title** tells you what is shown on the map.

**Step 2:** Look at the map key. The **map key** tells what the colors, pictures, and lines on a map mean.

**Step 3:** Find the compass rose. The **compass rose** shows the four **cardinal directions**. These are north (N), south (S), east (E), and west (W). It also shows **intermediate directions** that fall between the cardinal directions. They are northeast (NE), northwest (NW), southeast (SE), and southwest (SW).

**World Continents**

ARCTIC OCEAN

NORTH AMERICA

EUROPE

ASIA

PACIFIC OCEAN

ATLANTIC OCEAN

AFRICA

PACIFIC OCEAN

SOUTH AMERICA

INDIAN OCEAN

AUSTRALIA

**KEY**

ᐱᐱ Mountains

▢ Ocean

— River

N
NW    NE
W        E
SW    SE
S

SOUTHERN OCEAN

ANTARCTICA

## Practice the Skill

Use the map to answer these questions.

**1** Using the map key, tell what the curved blue line means.

**2** Which intermediate direction is between north and west?

**3** Use the compass rose to tell where Antarctica is in the world.

## Apply the Skill

Use the map above and the map on pages R6–R7 to answer these questions.

**1** In what ways are the two maps different?

**2** What continent is north of South America?

**3** Is Europe northwest or northeast of Australia?

15

# Lesson 2

# Communities and Resources

▶ **WHAT TO KNOW**
What resources do communities use?

▶ **VOCABULARY**

environment

natural resources

human resources

capital resources

region

**READING SKILL**
**Categorize** List the three categories of resources. Then give examples of each.

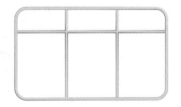

**Before You Read** What are your clothes made of? Your shirt or pants might be made of cotton. Cotton is one of the many things from nature that people use.

## Natural Resources

When you play outside, the sun warms you and the air around you. Air is part of your environment. The **environment** is the water, soil, air, and living things around you.

Plants are part of the environment. The fresh water in lakes and rivers is part of the environment, too. Plants and fresh water are natural resources. **Natural resources** are things found in nature that are useful to people. People use natural resources every day.

## Other Resources

People use three kinds of resources to make goods such as clothes. Natural resources are one kind. Human resources are another. **Human resources** are the skills, knowledge, and hard work that people bring to their jobs. Some workers know a lot about math. Others work very quickly and carefully. Other workers know how to use tools or machines.

**Capital resources** are things used by people to make goods or provide services. Machines, tools, buildings, and roads are examples of capital resources. The picture below shows how people use the three kinds of resources to grow and pick cotton.

**✓READING CHECK** CATEGORIZE A tractor is an example of what type of resource?

**Human Resources**
The work and skills of people, such as this driver, are human resources.

**Natural Resources**
These include the water and soil used to grow cotton plants.

**Capital Resources**
A spindle picker is a machine used to pick cotton.

17

# Regions and Resources

The resources people use may depend on the region where their community is located. A **region** is an area that shares one or more features. These features can include landforms, climate, and resources. For example, some communities are in sunny, warm regions. Others are in regions that have cold, wintry climates.

Communities use their resources in different ways. Limón (lee MOHN), Costa Rica, for example, is in a warm, sunny region. Its natural resources include good soil and sunshine. People in Limón use these resources to grow bananas they can sell all over the world.

*(main idea)*

New York City has its own resources, including the Hudson River and the Atlantic Ocean. These waterways make the city an ideal place for moving goods. More than eight million people live and work here. These natural and human resources have helped New York City become an important center for business.

**Water Resources** The Atlantic Ocean is an important resource for New York City.

## Conserving Natural Resources

Whether people live in small towns or large cities like New York City, they use many different kinds of resources. If people use too much of a natural resource, however, the resource may run out. People can conserve, or save, some kinds of natural resources.

One way to conserve natural resources is to reuse or recycle. Reusing means using something more than once. Recycling means making something new out of things that would have been thrown away. Can you think of something that you can reuse or recycle today?

**READING CHECK** DRAW CONCLUSIONS What resources might you use in a warm, sunny region?

**SUMMARY**

Natural resources, human resources, and capital resources are all used to make goods. Different communities use those resources in different ways.

## Lesson Review

❶ **WHAT TO KNOW** What resources do communities use?

❷ **VOCABULARY** Write a sentence using **natural resource** and **region**.

❸ **CRITICAL THINKING: Fact and Opinion** Of all the resources available to a big city like New York City, which do you think is the most important kind? Why?

❹ **ART ACTIVITY** Find out about resources used in your community. Make a poster showing one of each type of resource from your community.

❺ **READING SKILL** Complete the graphic organizer to categorize the three kinds of resources.

# Protecting Resources

**Whose job is it to care for the environment?**
People can help conserve natural resources so they don't run out. Today, as well as in the past, many people work to protect natural resources.

## John Muir
### (1838–1914)

As a young boy, John Muir (myur) explored the forest and countryside near his home in Scotland. In college, one of his favorite subjects was botany, or the study of plants. This led him to travel through Wisconsin, Iowa, and parts of Canada to learn more about plants.

Later, Muir took long journeys through other parts of our country. He lived for several years in the Yosemite Valley in California. He wrote articles about the need to care for and protect the natural resources of the valley. In 1890, United States leaders made Yosemite a national park.

## Marjory Stoneman Douglas
### (1890–1998)

Like John Muir, Marjory Stoneman Douglas loved the land around her. As a newspaper reporter, she wrote articles about the Florida Everglades and its alligators, pelicans, and panthers.

In a book, Douglas explained that the Everglades are like a big river. People began to understand the region better. The government made part of the Everglades a national park in 1947.

Douglas worked late into her life teaching people about the resources in the Everglades. She became known as the "Grandmother of the Glades."

## Activities

1. **THINK ABOUT IT** In what ways did John Muir and Marjory Stoneman Douglas show they cared for the land?

2. **PRESENT IT** Think about an outdoor place you love in your community. Write and present a short description of the natural resources found there.

# Looking at Culture

▶ **WHAT TO KNOW**
What are some parts
of culture?

▶ **VOCABULARY**

culture
tradition
needs
ethnic group

◎ **READING SKILL**
**Main Idea and Details**
As you read, fill in the
chart with details about
different parts of culture.

**Before You Read** What do people in your community do for fun? The things people enjoy are part of their culture.

## Ways of Life

The sports you play, the books you read, and the movies you watch are all part of your culture. **Culture** is the way of life a group of people share. It includes their ideas, beliefs, and languages. The music that people play or listen to is also part of their culture.

*main idea* ⭐

Culture also includes celebrations, art, and the lessons you learn in school. Even the clothes you wear and the food you eat are part of your culture.

**Music is part
of every culture.**

## Sharing Cultures

All cultures have beliefs and traditions. A **tradition** is a culture's special way of doing things. Adults pass down their traditions to children to keep their culture alive.

Holiday celebrations often involve many traditions. Families may eat special foods and sing certain songs at holiday celebrations. Some cultures have special dances that they perform on holidays. Adults teach children these traditions.

Children also learn about their culture through stories. Adults tell stories about important ideas or people from the past. Stories tell about a culture's traditions.

Adults pass down other traditions. They teach children about the language, religion, or rules of their culture.

**READING CHECK** MAIN IDEA AND DETAILS What is one way that children learn traditions of their culture?

**Families and Food** Children learn about traditional foods when sharing family meals.

# Comparing Cultures

People from all cultures have the same basic needs. **Needs** are the things people must have in order to live. Food, water, clothing, and shelter are basic needs. People often use resources found where they live to meet their needs.

Different cultures meet their needs in different ways. For example, all people need clothes. However, the clothes people wear differ from group to group. In hot, dry countries, such as Egypt, people wear light clothes that keep them cool all year. In colder countries such as Norway, people wear warm clothing in the winter.

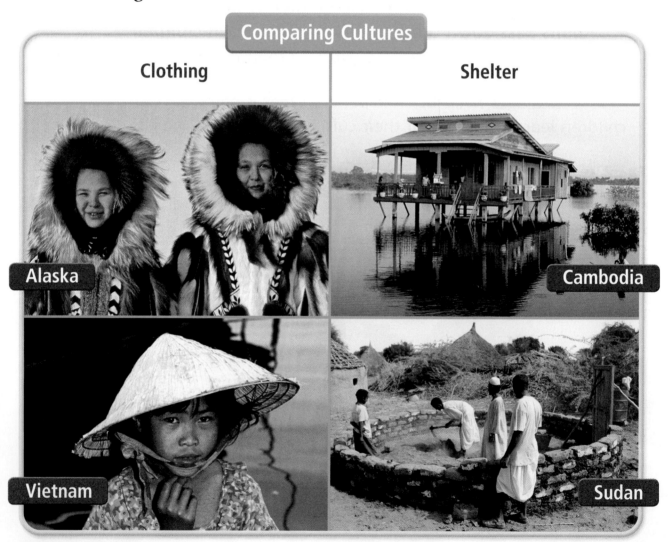

**Comparing Cultures**

**Clothing** | **Shelter**

Alaska

Cambodia

Vietnam

Sudan

**Meeting Needs** Weather affects how people meet basic needs.
**Skill** **Reading Charts** What do the pictures tell you about how these cultures meet needs?

## A Mix of Cultures

Different countries have different cultures. In some countries, most people belong to the same ethnic group. An **ethnic group** is a group of people who have their own language and culture. In these countries, most people share the same traditions and beliefs.

Other countries, such as the United States, have a mix of people from many ethnic groups. People bring the traditions of their ethnic group when they move to the United States. Traditions from many ethnic groups are now part of American culture. For example, Americans of all ethnic groups can eat Italian pizza and enjoy Brazilian music.

✔**READING CHECK** DRAW CONCLUSIONS In what ways are people from all cultures alike?

**SUMMARY**

Culture is the way of life a group of people share. Adults share their cultural traditions with children in many ways. Culture is different in different places.

## Lesson Review

**1 WHAT TO KNOW** What are some parts of culture?

**2 VOCABULARY** Use **tradition** in a sentence about culture.

**3 CRITICAL THINKING: Predict** What might happen when people from one ethnic group move to a new place?

**4 WRITING ACTIVITY** Write a list of questions you might ask someone from a different country about their culture.

**5 MAIN IDEA AND DETAILS** Complete the graphic organizer to show the main idea and details about different parts of culture.

# Language Regions of the World

**The language you speak is part of your culture.** You can learn a language from your family, your friends, or in school. Our world has about 5,000 languages.

This map shows major language families. A language family is a group of languages that are related. Each language in the family came from the same original language. But languages can change over time. As people travel, they bring languages and culture to new places.

English is part of the Indo-European language family. So are Portuguese, Spanish, and Italian. Look at the map and find all the places where people now speak Indo-European languages.

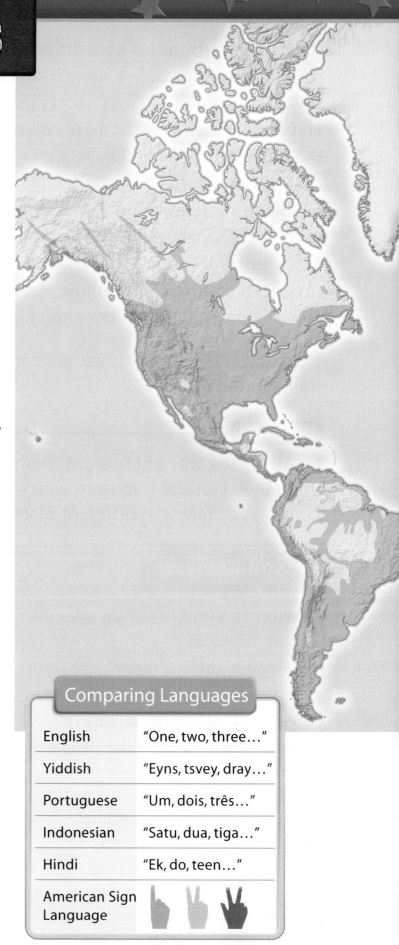

## Comparing Languages

| | |
|---|---|
| English | "One, two, three…" |
| Yiddish | "Eyns, tsvey, dray…" |
| Portuguese | "Um, dois, três…" |
| Indonesian | "Satu, dua, tiga…" |
| Hindi | "Ek, do, teen…" |
| American Sign Language | |

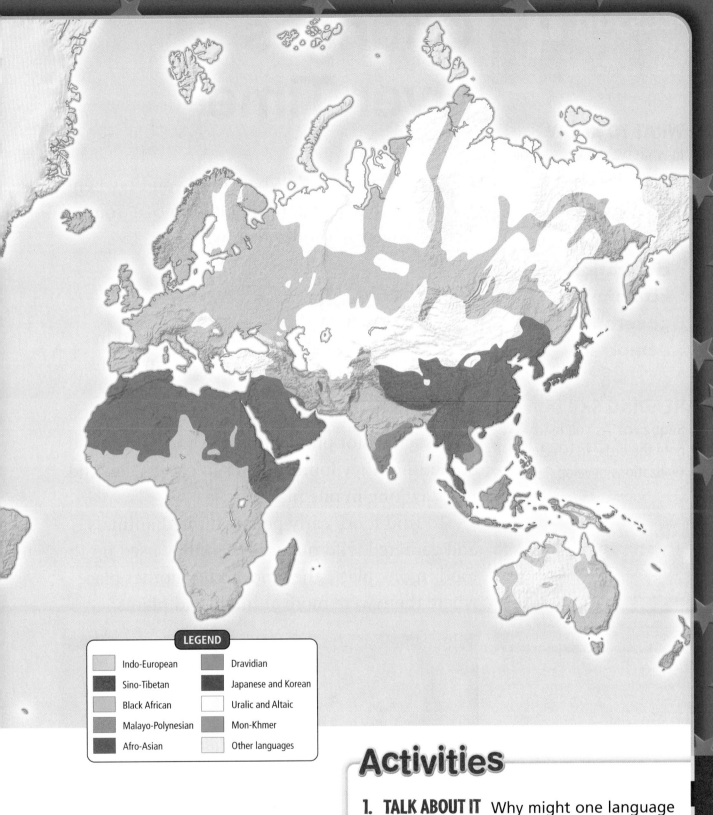

**LEGEND**

| | |
|---|---|
| Indo-European | Dravidian |
| Sino-Tibetan | Japanese and Korean |
| Black African | Uralic and Altaic |
| Malayo-Polynesian | Mon-Khmer |
| Afro-Asian | Other languages |

# Activities

1. **TALK ABOUT IT** Why might one language family be found in many countries?

2. **PRESENT IT** Find out what languages teachers and students at your school speak. Present your findings to the class.

# Changes Over Time

**WHAT TO KNOW**
In what ways have cultures changed over time?

**VOCABULARY**

agriculture
civilization
economy
government
democracy

**READING SKILL**
Sequence As you read, note the order in which civilizations develop.

**Before You Read** What could you do when you were a baby? What can you do now? You have changed as you have grown older.

## Early People

Over time, human culture has changed in many ways. Early people did not live in towns or cities. They lived in small, family groups. Groups lived far from each other. Early people built shelters for protection from the weather. Sometimes they found shelter in caves. They did not stay long in one place.

To find food, early people hunted animals and gathered wild plants. When they used up the food in one place, they moved to another place where there were more animals and plants.

*main idea*

About 15,000 years ago, early human beings painted pictures of animals they hunted on cave walls.

## Civilizations Begin

After a long time, people began practicing agriculture. **Agriculture** means growing crops and raising animals. Agriculture gave people a steady supply of food. It also caused big changes in the way people lived.

Crops need a lot of care and time to grow, so people began settling near their fields. They built houses meant to last and started communities. They grew extra crops for the future. This meant some people didn't have to farm. They learned new skills such as writing and making tools.

As people learned new skills, civilizations developed. A **civilization** is a group of people who live together with a shared culture, including writing, agriculture, science, and art. Civilizations grew after large numbers of people with different skills started living together in cities.

✓ **READING CHECK** SEQUENCE What happened after people began practicing agriculture?

**People in one early civilization wrote by making marks on soft clay. Only a few trained people, like those in the picture, knew how to write and read.**

# Changing the Land

Civilizations grew in different places and at different times. Civilizations change the places where they grow. For example, people may cut down forests to make farmland. They may also dig ditches to bring water to their crops. They use the natural resources around them to build homes and other structures.

**main idea** ★

Many civilizations that existed long ago have disappeared. New civilizations have grown where older civilizations once were. However, some structures built by early civilizations still exist. For example, over 3,000 years ago in north Africa, people in Egypt built huge stone pyramids. Ancient Egyptian civilization ended long ago, but you can still see the pyramids near the city of Cairo.

**The ancient pyramids stand near skyscrapers and apartment buildings in modern Cairo.**

pyramids

## Wagon

- In the 1860s, wagons heading west traveled on bumpy trails.

- Wagons traveled 1–2 miles per hour.

## Jet

- Jets today can carry more than 350 people.

- Jets can travel at about 600 miles per hour.

### Ways of Life Change

The ways people live also change over time. About 200 years ago, most people in the United States lived and worked on farms. The economy was based on growing food and selling what was left over. An **economy** is the way that people choose to make, buy, sell, and use things. When people traveled, they walked, rode horses, or used boats. They sent letters to communicate with people far away.

Today most Americans live in cities. They buy their food at stores. Many of the goods they use every day are grown or made in distant places. Most families travel in cars and fly in airplanes if they want to go long distances. Telephones and e-mail make it possible to communicate quickly with people far away.

✔ **READING CHECK** COMPARE AND CONTRAST How has communication changed in the United States over time?

# Government

Before civilizations developed, people lived in small groups. When larger numbers of people started living together in cities, they needed a way to keep order. They may also have had more conflicts than they did in small groups. People needed ways to get along with each other, so civilizations created governments. A **government** is a group of people who make laws, or rules, and keep order.

Many early civilizations were ruled by one person, such as a king. The United States, however, is a democracy. A **democracy** is a form of government in which the people make the decisions about how they should be ruled. In the United States, people choose leaders to make the laws.

In the United States, people vote for new leaders every few years.

## Governments Change

Governments change over time. They may change slowly and peacefully. They may also change by force. For example, the king of Great Britain once ruled America. Americans thought Great Britain treated them unfairly. On July 4, 1776, Americans created a new country, the United States. They wanted the new country to be a democracy. They fought a war with Great Britain to win their freedom and create a new government.

George Washington was our country's first President.

✓**READING CHECK** CLASSIFY What form of government does the United States have today?

**SUMMARY**

The people of a civilization share the same culture. Over time, civilizations and cultures change. Every civilization has a government.

## Lesson Review

**1 WHAT TO KNOW** In what ways have cultures changed over time?

**2 VOCABULARY** Use **democracy** in a sentence about government.

**3 CRITICAL THINKING: Draw Conclusions** Why was agriculture important to the start of civilizations?

**4 ART ACTIVITY** Draw two pictures to show how travel in the United States has changed over time.

**5 SEQUENCE** Complete the graphic organizer to show the order in which civilizations develop.

# Egyptian Hieroglyphics

**Have you written anything down today?** People write to communicate and to keep track of information. Like other parts of culture, the way people write has changed over time.

Today we use pencils and paper or computer keyboards to write words. The English alphabet has 26 letters with different sounds.

In ancient Egypt, people used hieroglyphics (hy uhr uh GLIHF ihks). Hieroglyphics is a kind of writing based on pictures and signs. Not everyone in Egypt could read or write hieroglyphics. Only special writers, called scribes, knew the signs and what they meant. At first, there were about 700 hieroglyphic signs, or hieroglyphs. Over time, Egyptians created more than 6,000 signs!

**Reed Brushes**
Scribes used reed brushes. The brushes and ink were kept in a wooden case.

**King Khufu**
These hieroglyphs stand for the name of King Khufu.

**Paper and Stone**
Scribes wrote on a type of paper called papyrus (puh PY ruhs). Some scribes also carved hieroglyphs onto temple walls.

# Activities

1. **THINK ABOUT IT** Look at the hieroglyphs that spell King Khufu's name. What signs look familiar to you?

2. **MAKE YOUR OWN** Design a hieroglyph that stands for you or your name.

 Visit Education Place for more primary sources. www.eduplace.com/nycssp/

# What's Wrong with This Map?

## Regions of Mexico

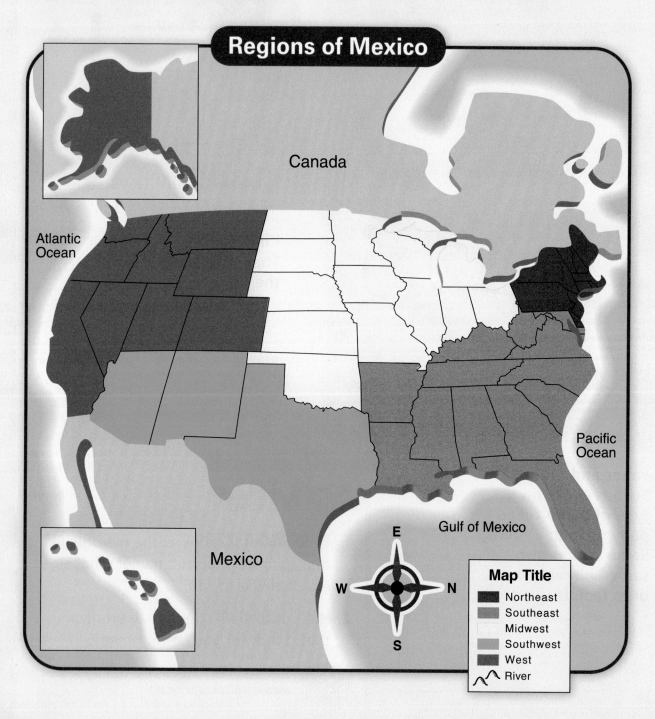

Canada

Atlantic Ocean

Pacific Ocean

Gulf of Mexico

Mexico

**Map Title**

- Northeast
- Southeast
- Midwest
- Southwest
- West
- River

# Figure It Out

Use the rebus to figure out each two-word term.

compass +  = ?

 + directions = ?

+ resource = ?

## Education Place®
www.eduplace.com

Go Digital

### Visit Eduplace!

Log on to Eduplace to explore Social Studies online. Solve puzzles to watch the skateboarding tricks in eWord Game. Join Chester in GeoNet to see if you can earn enough points to become a GeoChampion, or just play Wacky Web Tales to see how silly your stories can get. Play now at **www.eduplace.com/nycssp/**

World Communities Now and Long Ago
- eGlossary
- eWord Game
- Biographies
- Primary Sources
- Write Site
- Interactive Maps
- GeoGlossary
- GeoNet
- Online Atlas

# Review for Understanding

## Reading Social Studies

The **main idea** is the most important idea of a passage. **Details** are facts, reasons, or examples that support the main idea.

 **Main Idea and Details**

1. Complete this graphic organizer to show that you understand important details about how people use resources in the environment.

### Using Resources

Main Idea: People use resources from the environment to get the things they need.

| Detail | Detail | Detail |

 **Write About the Big Idea**

2. **Write a Paragraph** Culture, history, geography, people, and government are important features of communities throughout the world. Write a paragraph describing culture in your community. Include ethnic groups, languages, or cultural traditions that you see in the community around you.

## Vocabulary and Main Ideas

**Write a sentence to answer each question.**

3. What are some ways that people **adapt** to the **climate** where they live?

4. In what ways do people use **natural resources**?

5. What are some ways that adults share **culture** with children?

6. What kind of **government** do we have in the United States?

## Critical Thinking

**Write a short answer for each question. Use details to support your answer.**

7. **Cause and Effect** What might happen if people did not conserve resources?

8. **Predict** In what ways might your community change over the next 200 years?

## Apply Skills

**Use the map of New York State to answer each question.**

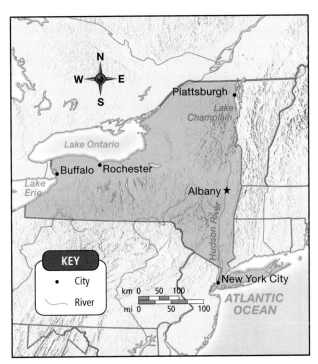

9. Using the map key, tell what a black dot means.

10. What direction is New York City from Albany?

   **A.** east

   **B.** west

   **C.** north

   **D.** south

# Unit 1 Activities

 ## Unit Writing Activity

**Write a Story** Write a story about a cultural tradition that your family celebrates.

■ Include foods you eat, clothes you wear, or other parts of the tradition.

■ Describe why this tradition is special to you.

 ## Unit Project

**Nature Center Exhibit** Create a nature exhibit that tells about a community in the United States.

■ Describe the climate, land, water, and natural resources.

■ Show information on posters.

## Read More

■ *Earth and You—A Closer View: Nature's Features* by Patrick J. Lewis. Dawn Publications, 2004.

■ *If the World Were a Village: A Book About the World's People* by David J. Smith. A & C Black Publishers Ltd., 2004.

■ *The Voice of the People: American Democracy in Action* by Betsy Maestro. HarperTrophy, 1998.

**Go Digital** visit www.eduplace.com/nycssp/

# Africa

**Victoria Falls on the Zambezi River**

How do culture, history, geography, people, and government affect communities in Africa?

## WHAT TO KNOW

✓ What are some of Africa's geographic features?

✓ How do people in Nigeria use natural resources?

✓ What are some key events in Nigeria's history?

✓ What are some cultural traditions in Nigeria?

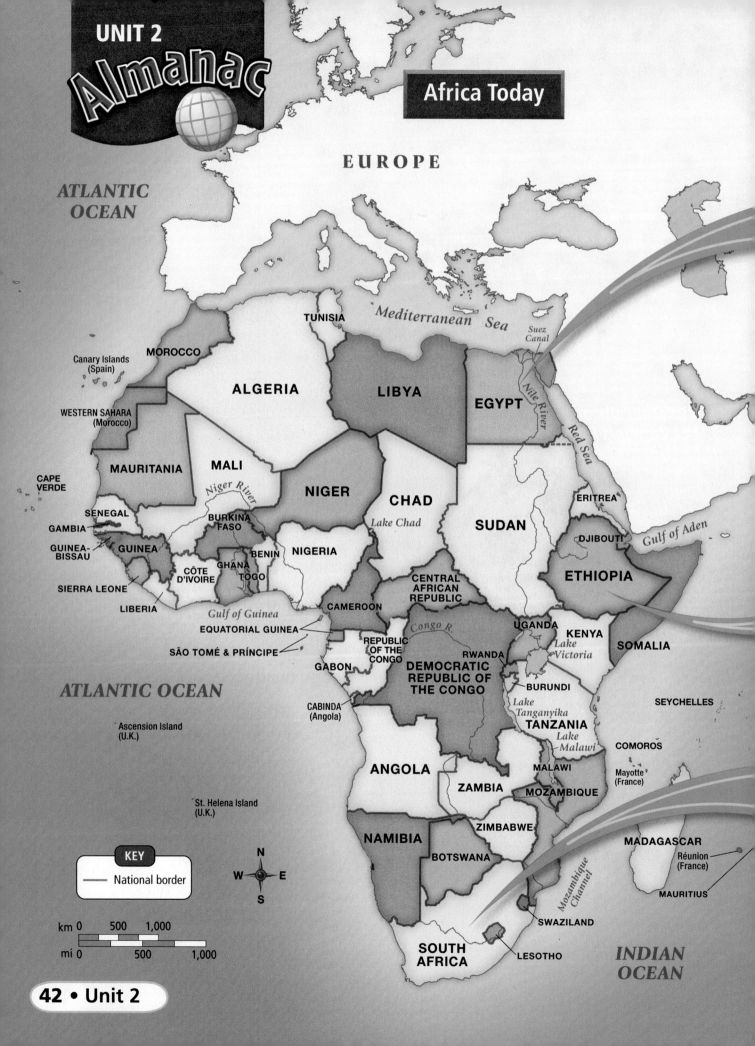

ATLANTIC
OCEAN

EUROPE

Mediterranean Sea

TUNISIA

MOROCCO

Canary Islands
(Spain)

ALGERIA

LIBYA

Suez
Canal

EGYPT

Nile River

Red Sea

WESTERN SAHARA
(Morocco)

CAPE
VERDE

MAURITANIA

MALI

Niger River

NIGER

CHAD

Lake Chad

SUDAN

ERITREA

Gulf of Aden

DJIBOUTI

SENEGAL

GAMBIA

BURKINA
FASO

GUINEA-
BISSAU

GUINEA

BENIN

NIGERIA

CÔTE
D'IVOIRE

GHANA
TOGO

SIERRA LEONE

LIBERIA

Gulf of Guinea

CAMEROON

EQUATORIAL GUINEA

SÃO TOMÉ & PRÍNCIPE

GABON

CABINDA
(Angola)

CENTRAL
AFRICAN
REPUBLIC

Congo R.

REPUBLIC
OF THE
CONGO

ETHIOPIA

UGANDA

KENYA

Lake
Victoria

SOMALIA

RWANDA

DEMOCRATIC
REPUBLIC OF
THE CONGO

BURUNDI

Lake
Tanganyika

TANZANIA

Lake
Malawi

SEYCHELLES

COMOROS

ATLANTIC OCEAN

Ascension Island
(U.K.)

St. Helena Island
(U.K.)

ANGOLA

ZAMBIA

MALAWI

MOZAMBIQUE

Mayotte
(France)

ZIMBABWE

MADAGASCAR

Réunion
(France)

NAMIBIA

BOTSWANA

Mozambique Channel

MAURITIUS

SWAZILAND

SOUTH
AFRICA

LESOTHO

INDIAN
OCEAN

Boys in Egypt

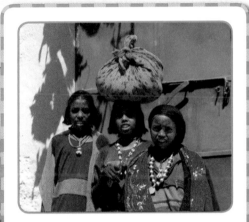

Girls in Ethiopia

*INDIAN OCEAN*

Family in South Africa

# Connect to
# The World

## African Countries with the Most People

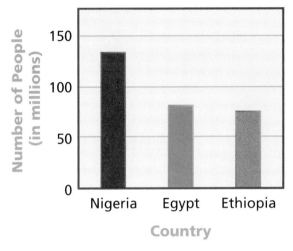

## Top Winners of the Africa Cup of Nations

= 1 first-place win

Egypt   Cameroon   Ghana   Nigeria

Soccer is very popular in Africa. Every two years, 16 countries compete for the Africa Cup of Nations.

• Which countries appear in both graphs?
• Which country has won the Africa Cup of Nations most often?

# Reading Social Studies
## Compare and Contrast

**Why It Matters** To compare and contrast people, ideas, and things is to tell how they are alike and different.

## Learn the Skill

To **compare** things is to tell how they are alike, or similar.
To **contrast** things is to tell how they are different.

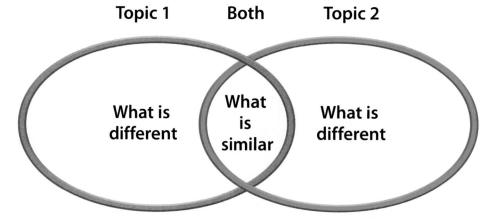

| Topic 1 | Both | Topic 2 |

What is different — What is similar — What is different

- Words and phrases, such as *the same as, like, both,* and *similar,* are clues that two things are being compared.

- Words and phrases, such as *different from, unlike, however,* and *but,* are clues that two things are being contrasted.

## Practice the Skill

**Read the paragraph. Then compare and contrast.**

`Contrast` Lagos is in Nigeria, in Africa. Washington, D.C., is in the
`Compare` United States, in North America. Lagos and Washington, D.C., are both large, busy cities. However, they grew differently.

# Apply the Skill

**Read the paragraphs, and answer the questions.**

## Lagos and Washington, D.C.

Washington, D.C., is the capital of the United States. Lagos used to be the capital of Nigeria. These cities are very different in many ways. Yet they are alike in many ways, too.

Both cities are good places to buy and sell things because they are near water. Lagos is near the Gulf of Guinea. Washington, D.C., is mainly next to the Potomac River. Boats can carry people and things to and from cities that are near water.

**Washington, D.C.**

The two cities grew in different ways. Lagos grew fast. It was not planned to become a large capital city. Washington, D.C., was planned to be the United States capital.

Today, Lagos and Washington, D.C., share large-city problems. Both need more homes and better ways for people to travel around the city.

**Lagos**

## Compare and Contrast

**1.** How are Washington, D.C., and Lagos alike?

**2.** How are these cities different?

**3.** What problems do both cities have in common today?

# Vocabulary Preview

## endangered

The African mountain gorilla is in danger of dying out. Wildlife parks help protect these **endangered** animals.

**page 52**

## industry

Producing oil is Nigeria's biggest **industry.** This industry is made up of all the people and companies that drill for, prepare, and sell oil. **page 58**

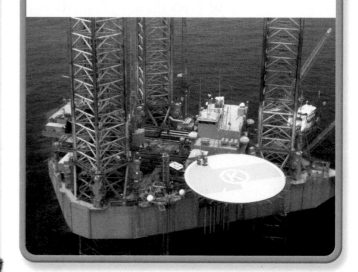

# Reading Strategy

**Summarize** Use the Summarize strategy in Lessons 1 and 2.

**Predict and Infer** Use the Predict and Infer strategy in Lessons 3 and 4.

## artifact

An **artifact** tells us about the culture of the people who made it. Many of these objects have been found in Nigeria.

**page 66**

## artisan

A person who makes arts and crafts is an **artisan.** Nigeria has many of these skilled workers who make goods by hand.

**page 76**

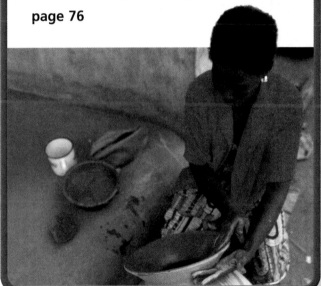

**Go Digital** visit www.eduplace.com/nycssp/

# Study Skills

## MAKE AN OUTLINE

An outline organizes topics, main ideas, and details.

- Topics are shown by Roman numerals.

- Main ideas about each topic are shown by capital letters.

- Details about each main idea are shown by numbers.

## Africa

I. This Is Africa
   A. Africa has many kinds of land and water.
      1. There are mountains, deserts, savannas, and rain forests.
      2.
   B. Africa has a variety of climates, plants, animals, and resources.
      1. Regions can be dry or rainy.
      2.

# Lesson 1 — This Is Africa

## WHAT TO KNOW
What are some of Africa's geographic features?

## VOCABULARY
canal
savanna
rain forest
endangered

## READING SKILL
**Compare and Contrast**
As you read, compare and contrast Africa's desert and rain forest climates.

**Before You Read** Think of one kind of landform or body of water. There are deserts, mountains, forests, lakes, rivers, and many others. Almost any geographic feature you can name is found in Africa.

## The Many Countries of Africa

Africa is the world's second-largest continent. It is made up of more than 50 countries! A country is an area with its own people and laws. Each country in Africa has its own geography, history, government, and cultures.

If you explored all of Africa's countries, you would see amazing sights. These include the world's largest desert, the Sahara, and the world's longest river, the Nile. Other features you would see are deep valleys, snowy mountains, thick forests, and vast plains. Many countries also have large lakes and powerful rivers and waterfalls.

**Mount Kilimanjaro** This peak in Tanzania is Africa's highest mountain.

## Land and Water

If you look at the map on page 51, you will see that Africa has many physical features. Mountains, hills, plateaus, and plains appear throughout the continent. There are large deserts in the north and south. To the east is the Great Rift Valley. Here rifts, or cracks in the land, form deep valleys with steep sides.

Africa has many waterways. They both connect and separate people and countries. The Nile River begins at Lake Victoria and flows north through nine countries until it flows into the Mediterranean Sea. The Suez Canal was built to join the Mediterranean and the Red seas. A **canal** is a waterway made by people.

Other major rivers are the Congo, Niger, and Zambezi. Victoria Falls, one of the biggest waterfalls in the world, is on the Zambezi. Many of Africa's large lakes are in the Great Rift Valley.

**The Great Rift Valley** This area in East Africa has many volcanoes and lakes.

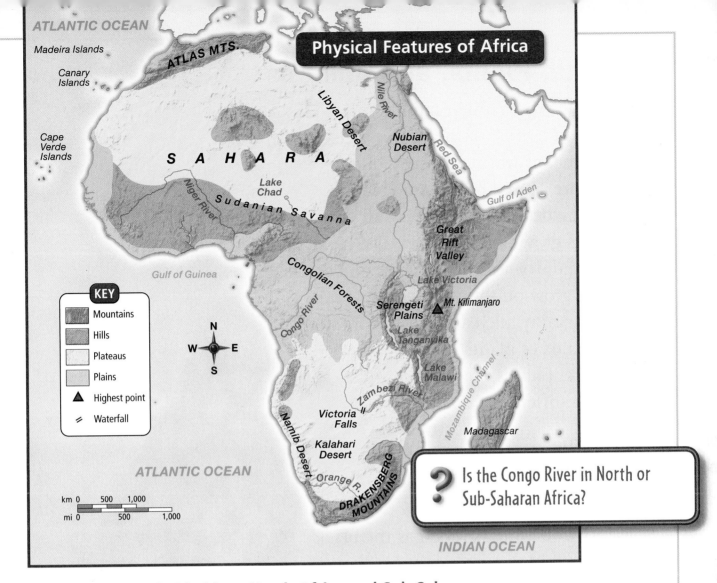

## Physical Features of Africa

ATLANTIC OCEAN

Madeira Islands

Canary Islands

Cape Verde Islands

ATLAS MTS.

SAHARA

Libyan Desert

Nile River

Nubian Desert

Red Sea

Gulf of Aden

Niger River

Lake Chad

Sudanian Savanna

Gulf of Guinea

Congolian Forests

Congo River

Great Rift Valley

Lake Victoria

Serengeti Plains

Mt. Kilimanjaro

Lake Tanganyika

Lake Malawi

Mozambique Channel

Zambezi River

Victoria Falls

Madagascar

Namib Desert

Kalahari Desert

Orange R.

DRAKENSBERG MOUNTAINS

ATLANTIC OCEAN

INDIAN OCEAN

**KEY**
- Mountains
- Hills
- Plateaus
- Plains
- ▲ Highest point
- Waterfall

N W E S

km 0   500   1,000
mi 0   500   1,000

**?** Is the Congo River in North or Sub-Saharan Africa?

Africa can be divided into North Africa and Sub-Saharan Africa. Sub-Saharan means "south of the Sahara."

## Different Kinds of Environments

Africa has different environments. The Sahara, a dry sandy desert, covers most of North Africa. South of the desert, savanna stretches across Africa. A **savanna** is land with tall grass and few trees.

There are rain forests in central Africa. A **rain forest** is a forest that has many trees and gets lots of rain. The Congolian Forests are one of Africa's largest rain forest regions. To the east and south of the rain forests is more savanna. The Serengeti Plains are a large savanna in this region. Further south are the dry Namib and Kalahari deserts.

✓**READING CHECK** COMPARE AND CONTRAST How are the savanna and the rain forest alike? How are they different?

# Climate, Plants, and Animals

Though Africa's high mountain peaks have cool temperatures, most of the continent has a tropical climate. Tropical means warm all year. Differences in Africa's climates are caused by the amount of rainfall in each region. The deserts are very dry all year. Without rain, few plants grow in the deserts. The savannas have rainy seasons and dry seasons. Grasses and some shrubs and trees grow on the savannas. The rain forests are rainy all year round. More than 25,000 kinds of plants grow there!

Different kinds of wildlife live in Africa's different climate regions. Lions, zebras, giraffes, ostriches, and elephants roam the savannas. Gorillas, chimpanzees, and African grey parrots make their home in the rain forests. Some African animals, such as the black rhinoceros and the mountain gorilla, are endangered. An **endangered** plant or animal is one that is in danger of dying out.

**Wildlife Parks** Many African countries are creating wildlife parks to protect endangered animals, such as these mountain gorillas.

## Natural Resources

Many people in African countries grow their own food. The rich soil found in some regions in Africa is an important resource for growing crops. In drier areas of Africa where the soil is poor, farmers use the land to raise animals. People in certain African countries also harvest trees from forests to sell wood.

Africa is rich in mineral resources. A mineral is a natural resource that is mined, or dug out of the ground. The country of South Africa is famous for its diamonds and gold. Oil is an important resource in northern and western Africa. Copper, iron, and cobalt are also found in Africa.

**Ebony** The special dark wood of ebony trees is a valuable resource in East Africa.

✔**READING CHECK** MAIN IDEA AND DETAILS What are some of Africa's natural resources?

**SUMMARY**

Africa is a large continent with more than 50 countries. It has both wet and dry climates and many kinds of land, water, plants, animals, and resources.

## Lesson Review

❶ **WHAT TO KNOW** What are some of Africa's geographic features?

❷ **VOCABULARY** Use **endangered** in a sentence about the **rain forest.**

❸ **CRITICAL THINKING: Infer** Name some jobs people could do using Africa's natural resources.

❹ **ART ACTIVITY** Draw or copy a map of Africa. Label areas as *desert*, *savanna*, or *rain forest*.

❺ **COMPARE AND CONTRAST** Complete the graphic organizer to compare and contrast Africa's desert and rain forest climates.

Africa's Desert Climate    Similar    Africa's Rain Forest Climate

very rainy

# Skillbuilder

# Read a Map Scale

**VOCABULARY**

map scale

To see Africa's countries, you could travel from city to city. How could you find out how far each city is from another? You could use a map scale. A map scale helps you to measure distance.

## Learn the Skill

km 0    500    1,000
mi 0          500          1,000

**Step 1:** Look at the map scale. It shows that 1 inch on the map stands for 1,000 miles in the real world.

**Step 2:** Use a ruler to find the distance between the cities of Cape Town and Maputo on the map. The ruler measures 1 inch, so the distance between these two places is about 1,000 miles.

**Step 3:** For longer distances, multiply the number of inches by 1,000 miles. For example, suppose you measure 2 inches between the places on the map. When you multiply 2 times 1,000, you get 2,000 miles.

## Practice the Skill

Use a ruler and the map scale to answer the questions.

**1** About how many miles is it from Lagos to Cairo?

**2** About how many miles is it from Cairo to Lusaka?

**3** Which is shorter, the distance between Accra and Johannesburg or the distance between Abuja and Lusaka?

Cities in Africa

Cairo ⊛
EGYPT

AFRICA

NIGERIA
⊛ Abuja
GHANA   Lagos •
⊛
Accra

ATLANTIC
OCEAN

N
W ⊛ E
S

INDIAN
OCEAN

ZAMBIA
Lusaka ⊛   MOZAMBIQUE

KEY
• City
⊛ Capital city

km 0   500   1,000
mi 0    500    1,000

Johannesburg •   ⊛ Maputo

SOUTH
AFRICA
Cape Town ⊛

## Apply the Skill

Turn to the political map of the United States on pages R8
and R9. Using the scale, find the distance between the following
cities on the map:

❶ Columbus, Ohio, and Tampa, Florida

❷ Phoenix, Arizona, and San Diego, California

▶ **WHAT TO KNOW**
How do people in Nigeria use natural resources?

▶ **VOCABULARY**
   delta
   industry
   manufacturing
   urban
   rural

**READING SKILL**
**Cause and Effect** As you read, list ways Nigeria's land and resources affect the country.

# NIGERIA
## Land and Economy

Africa can be divided into four regions: North, South, East, and West Africa. Nigeria is a country in West Africa, on the Gulf of Guinea, which is a part of the Atlantic Ocean.

Nigeria gets its name from the country's major river, the Niger. The Niger Delta is formed where the river meets the ocean. A **delta** is a triangle of sand and soil deposited by a river. The Niger Delta is rich in natural resources.

**The Niger** Many Nigerians use the Niger River for transportation.

## Climate and Resources

Nigeria has different kinds of climates and resources. The entire country is warm all year, and it has a rainy season and a dry season. However, the climates in the north and south have some differences. It is hotter and drier in the northern savannas, hills, and plateaus than in the southern rain forests and wetlands. More rain falls in the south, and the temperature is milder because this area is closer to the ocean.

main idea

Nigeria's resources include rich soil, forests, and fish in its rivers and lakes. The country also has many minerals, such as coal, iron ore, tin, gold, and columbite, which is used to make steel. Nigeria's greatest resource is oil. Oil is found in the south and offshore in the Gulf of Guinea.

✓**READING CHECK** CAUSE AND EFFECT How does the ocean affect temperature in Nigeria?

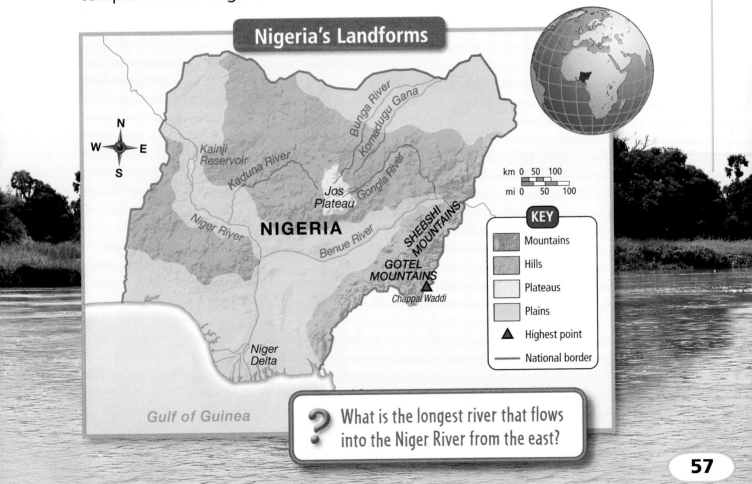

**Nigeria's Landforms**

Bunga River
Komadugu Gana
Kainji Reservoir
Kaduna River
Gongla River
Jos Plateau
Niger River
**NIGERIA**
Benue River
SHEBSHI MOUNTAINS
GOTEL MOUNTAINS
Chappal Waddi
Niger Delta
Gulf of Guinea

km 0 50 100
mi 0 50 100

**KEY**
Mountains
Hills
Plateaus
Plains
▲ Highest point
— National border

? What is the longest river that flows into the Niger River from the east?

57

## Nigeria's Economy

*main idea* ⭐

Nigeria's economy depends on its natural resources. Most Nigerians are farmers. They use the country's rich soil to grow crops and use grassy land to raise animals. People also get fish from rivers, lakes, and the ocean.

Many other Nigerians work in the oil industry. An **industry** is all the companies and people that make or sell one kind of product or service. Producing oil is Nigeria's most important industry. Nigeria is one of the largest oil producers in the world.

Some people in Nigeria work in the manufacturing industry. **Manufacturing** is the making of products with machines. Nigeria manufactures items such as steel, clothing, lumber, and chemicals.

Nigerians trade many of the goods that they farm, manufacture, and mine. To trade is to buy and sell goods or services. Nigerians trade with each other and with other countries.

✔**READING CHECK** SUMMARIZE What kinds of activities are important to Nigeria's economy?

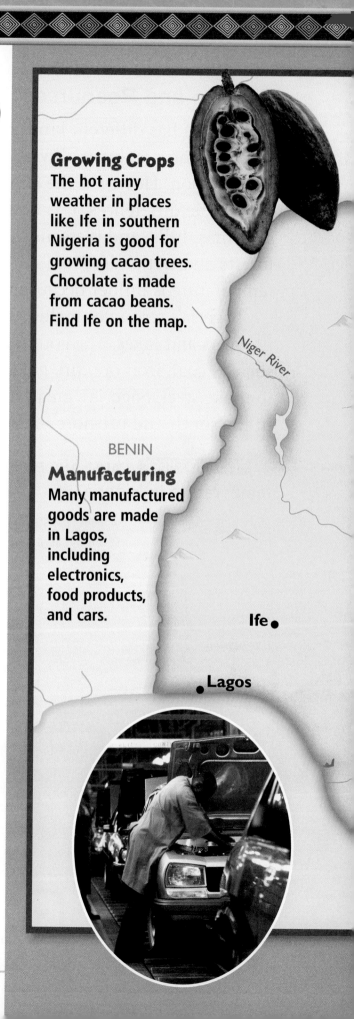

**Growing Crops**
The hot rainy weather in places like Ife in southern Nigeria is good for growing cacao trees. Chocolate is made from cacao beans. Find Ife on the map.

Niger River

BENIN

**Manufacturing**
Many manufactured goods are made in Lagos, including electronics, food products, and cars.

Ife •

• Lagos

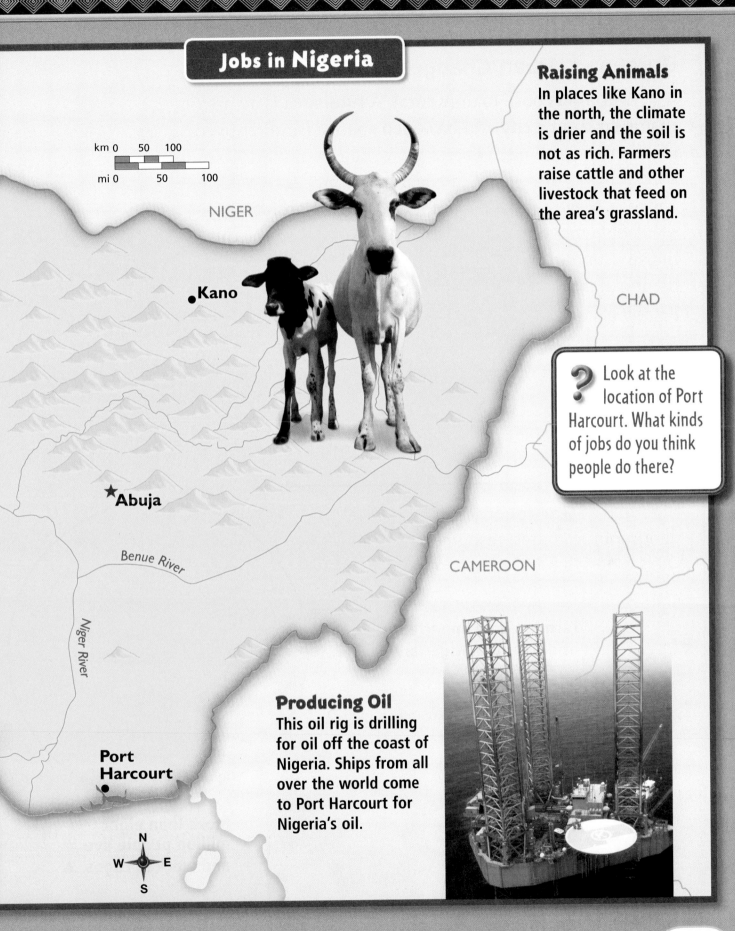

## Jobs in Nigeria

**Raising Animals**
In places like Kano in the north, the climate is drier and the soil is not as rich. Farmers raise cattle and other livestock that feed on the area's grassland.

km 0    50    100
mi 0      50    100

NIGER

CHAD

.Kano

? Look at the location of Port Harcourt. What kinds of jobs do you think people do there?

★Abuja

Benue River

CAMEROON

Niger River

**Producing Oil**
This oil rig is drilling for oil off the coast of Nigeria. Ships from all over the world come to Port Harcourt for Nigeria's oil.

Port Harcourt
●

N
W    E
S

## Rural and Urban Changes

Nigeria was once mainly rural. A **rural** area is an area that is far from a city and has open spaces. Families lived together in small villages and grew their own food. Then, in 1956, oil was discovered in Nigeria. Oil production became Nigeria's biggest industry, but it also caused problems.

People moved to urban areas to take jobs in the oil industry and other industries. An **urban** area is a city. Family life in rural areas changed as people left farms. With fewer people farming, there was less food for Nigeria's people. To solve this problem, Nigerian farmers learned better ways to farm and produce more food.

✔**READING CHECK** COMPARE AND CONTRAST How is life in urban areas different from life in rural areas in Nigeria?

**SUMMARY**

Nigeria is a large country with different kinds of geography, climates, resources, and industries. Oil is Nigeria's most important resource.

**Farming is an important part of life in rural Nigeria.** ▼

**More than eight million people live and work in Lagos.** ▲

### ❶ What to Know

How do people in Nigeria use natural resources?

### ❷ Reading Skill  Cause and Effect

Complete the graphic organizer to show cause-and-effect relationships.

Nigeria is rich in oil. →

### ❸ Case Study Detective

This is a photograph of the Niger Delta. Find the Niger Delta on the map on page 57. How do you think the many waterways affect transportation in Nigeria?

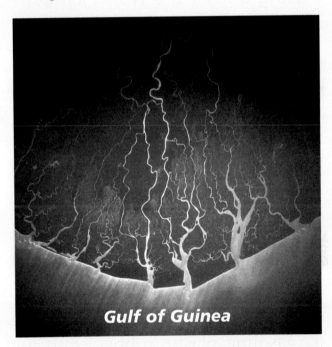

Gulf of Guinea

### ❹ Word Play

A *harmattan* is a hot, dry wind that enters Nigeria from the Sahara to the north. Look at some words that can be made from the letters in *harmattan*. How many more can you make?

an   _____   _____
ham  _____   _____
rat  _____   _____

# Nigeria's Oil

**Every day, you use products that are made using one of the world's most important natural resources: oil.**

Petroleum is oil found underground and under the ocean floor. It comes from plants and animals that lived millions of years ago. Over time, their remains slowly turned into a liquid. This liquid is petroleum. It can be a clear, light liquid. Or, it can be as dark and thick as molasses.

Oil from Nigeria's delta region is used all around the world. Nigeria produces more than two million barrels every day! This oil is used to make gasoline, plastic, rubber, cloth, and many other goods. The chart shows how Nigeria's oil is turned into gasoline.

At oil refineries, oil is broken down and treated to make different kinds of fuels and chemicals. These substances can be used to make other products.

## From Oil to Gasoline

**❶ Drilling Oil**

Oil wells drill deep into the ground and pump oil to the surface. There are also oil wells built in the ocean that pump oil from beneath the sea.

**❷ Refining Oil**

The oil goes to a factory called a refinery. At the refinery the oil is heated. This causes oil to separate into different substances, including gasoline.

**❸ Moving Oil**

Gasoline and other products prepared at the refinery are carried around the world by pipes, trucks, railroads, and ships.

**❹ Buying Gasoline**

Trucks deliver gasoline to gas stations. People use the gasoline to power cars, buses, trucks, and boats.

## Activities

1. **DRAW IT** Draw a picture that shows one way you and your family use oil.

2. **WRITE IT** Explain how your everyday life would be different without oil.

# Read a History Timeline

Graph and Chart Skills

▶ **VOCABULARY**

timeline

decade

century

millennium

Timelines help people organize important events in history. A timeline shows the dates of past events and the order in which they occurred.

## Learn the Skill

A timeline can be divided by years, decades, or even centuries. A **decade** is a period of 10 years. A **century** is 100 years. Timelines showing events from very long ago are often divided into periods of one or two thousand years. A period of one thousand years is called a **millennium**.

**Step 1:** Look at the first and last dates on the timeline to see the time period covered.

**Step 2:** Read the label B.C.E., which stands for Before Common Era. These dates show events that took place before the year 1. The oldest dates are on the left. An event that happened in 200 B.C.E. took place before the year 100 B.C.E.

**Step 3:** Read the label C.E., which stands for Common Era. These dates show events that took place between the year C.E. 1 and the present time. For example, an event that happened in C.E. 200 took place after the year C.E. 100.

| 4000 B.C.E. | 3000 B.C.E. | 2000 B.C.E. | 1000 B.C.E. | B.C.E. | C.E. | C.E. 1000 | C.E. 2000 |

## Practice the Skill

Use the timeline above to answer the questions.

**1** Which end of the timeline shows the most recent dates?

**2** How many years are shown on the timeline?

**3** Which year is more recent, 4000 B.C.E. or C.E. 2000?

## Apply the Skill

Copy the timeline onto a piece of paper. Then place each event below in its correct place on the timeline.

500 B.C.E.    **The Nok people begin to build communities in northern Nigeria.**

C.E. 1000    **The Yoruba people begin to build communities in southern Nigeria.**

C.E. 1472    **European explorers arrive in Nigeria.**

C.E. _____    **I am born.**

**This container is about 400 years old.**

65

# NIGERIA
## History and Government

► **WHAT TO KNOW**
What are some key events in Nigeria's history?

► **VOCABULARY**

artifact
slavery
colony
independence
capital

**READING SKILL**

**Sequence** As you read, list in order events that occurred during and after British rule in Nigeria.

People have lived in the area that is now Nigeria for thousands of years. How can we learn about people who lived so long ago? One way is to study artifacts. An **artifact** is an object that tells us about the culture of the people who made it. The clay artifact on this page was made by a group called the Nok. They lived in Nigeria from about 500 B.C.E. to C.E. 200.

Artifacts made of bronze metal have also been found in Nigeria. Some were made by a group called the Igbo (EE boh). The Igbo still live in Nigeria.

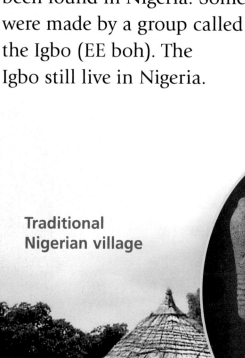

Traditional
Nigerian village

Nok Statue

## Northern and Southern Kingdoms

Beginning around C.E. 1000, different groups of people formed kingdoms in Nigeria. A kingdom is a country ruled by a king or queen. The Hausa (HOW suh) built kingdoms in the north. Hausa farmers, weavers, and leatherworkers traded with each other and with people from faraway kingdoms.

In the southwest, the Yoruba (YOHR uh buh) created the city of Ife (EE fay) and later, the kingdom of Oyo (OH yoh). Nearby, the Edo created the kingdom of Benin (buh NEEN). Both civilizations made bronze, brass, and ivory sculptures.

In the southeast, thick forests kept the Igbo from forming large kingdoms. This group of traders and skilled artists lived in small villages instead.

Benin bronze sculpture

✓ **READING CHECK** SEQUENCE Which came first, Ife or Oyo?

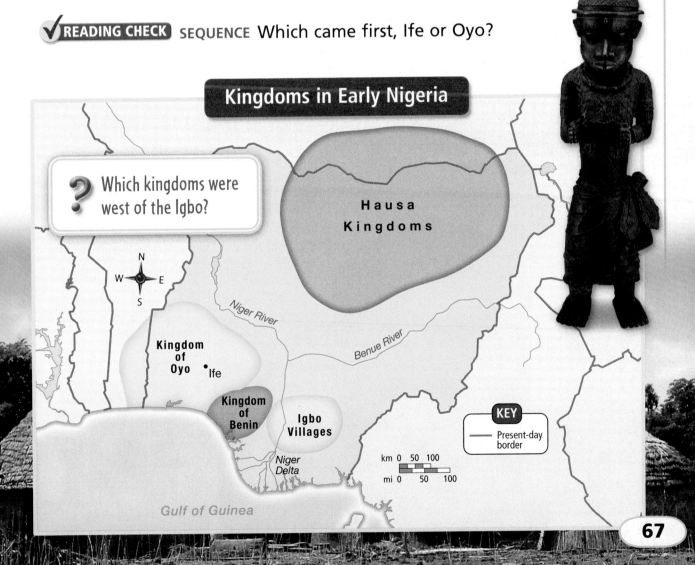

**Kingdoms in Early Nigeria**

? Which kingdoms were west of the Igbo?

Hausa Kingdoms

Niger River

Kingdom of Oyo • Ife

Benue River

Kingdom of Benin

Igbo Villages

KEY
— Present-day border

km 0 50 100
mi 0 50 100

Niger Delta

Gulf of Guinea

## From Colony to Democracy

People in Nigeria continued to live in different groups and kingdoms for hundreds of years. In the late 1400s, people from Europe started coming to Nigeria. Most of these people came to make money by selling Nigerians into slavery. **Slavery** is a cruel system in which people have no freedom and are forced to work without pay.

More than 300 years later, people from the country of Great Britain began exploring Nigeria in search of natural resources to trade. They took over the trading port of Lagos in southern Nigeria and made it into a colony. A **colony** is an area under another country's control. The British then began taking over more regions in Nigeria to control trade. In 1914 all of Nigeria became one British colony.

## NIGERIA'S HISTORY

| 1000 | 1250 | 1500 |
|------|------|------|

**About c.e. 1000**
The Yoruba create the city of Ife.

**1472**
Europeans begin arriving in Nigeria.

## Independence

During Britain's control of Nigeria, Nigerians worked to have more say in their government. By 1960, Nigeria had gained its independence from Britain. **Independence** means freedom from someone else's control. A new government was formed. However, the country did not have good leaders in the years that followed. Nigerians had little freedom, and different groups fought each other for control of the government.

Nigerians have worked for many years to become an independent and peaceful democracy. In a democracy, people vote to choose their leaders. In 1999, Nigerians elected Olusegun Obasanjo (oh LOO see gun oh BAH sahn joh) as their president. Nigeria has continued to have free elections since then.

*main idea*

✔**READING CHECK** CAUSE AND EFFECT Why did people from Europe first come to Nigeria?

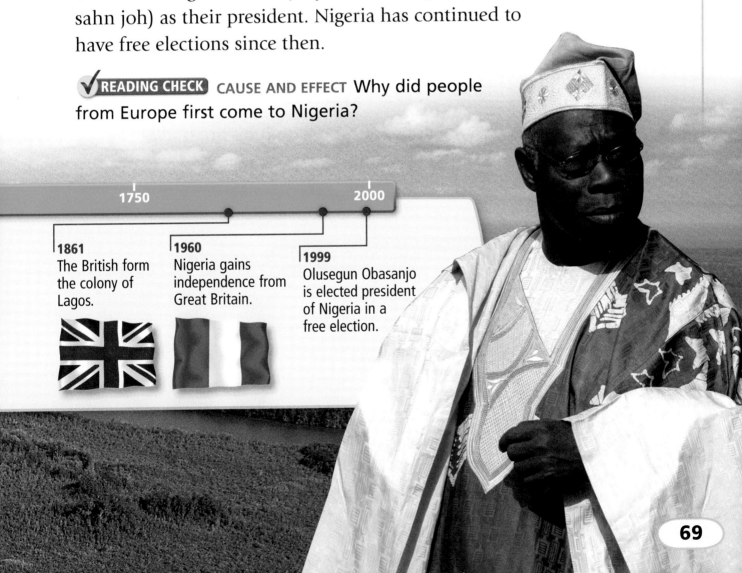

1750

2000

**1861**
The British form the colony of Lagos.

**1960**
Nigeria gains independence from Great Britain.

**1999**
Olusegun Obasanjo is elected president of Nigeria in a free election.

## Government Today

Nigeria has a government similar to the United States' government. It has three parts—a president, lawmakers, and judges. The president leads the country and chooses people called ministers to help. Lawmakers are members of either the Senate or the House of Representatives. There are judges at different levels of courts, including a Supreme Court.

Nigeria is made up of 36 states. Like the states in the United States, each one has its own leader and lawmakers.

Abuja (ah BOO juh) is the capital of Nigeria. A **capital** is the city where a state or country's government is located. Like Washington, D.C., Abuja is a planned city. It was built in the center of Nigeria to help unite the country's different regions.

**✔ READING CHECK** COMPARE AND CONTRAST Name three ways the governments of Nigeria and the United States are alike.

**SUMMARY** ─────────────────────────────

There were different groups of people and kingdoms in Nigeria long ago. Later Nigeria became a colony of Great Britain. Now it is an independent democracy.

### Nigeria's Government

**Lawmakers**
• Pass new laws

**President**
• Leads the government
• Asks lawmakers to pass laws
• Plans how money is to be spent

**Judges**
• Interpret laws
• Settle disagreements

**Skill** Reading Charts
Who interprets laws in Nigeria?

# CASE STUDY REVIEW

## ❶ What to Know
What are some key events in Nigeria's history?

## ❷ Reading Skill  Sequence
Complete the graphic organizer to sequence events.

> The British form the colony of Lagos.
>
> ↓
>
> [ ]
>
> ↓
>
> [ ]

## ❸ Case Study Detective 🔍

What do you think this modern artifact might tell people in the future about our culture?

## ❹ Word Play
Unscramble the letters to find the name of each group.

- They lived in the southeast.  BIGO

- They built kingdoms in the north.  ASAHU

- They created the kingdom of Oyo.  BOARUY

# Royal Art of BENIN

**What is your favorite animal?**
In the kingdom of Benin long ago, artists created statues of leopards, snakes, and other animals. These animals reminded people of their king, called the *oba*. The animal statues showed that the oba was powerful like a leopard and fierce like a snake.

Artists in Benin used long-lasting materials such as ivory, brass, and bronze. The artwork decorated the walls of the oba's palace in Benin City.

Today, many Yoruba communities still have an oba. Obas don't rule Nigeria, but they are still highly respected leaders in the community. Artists continue to make objects to honor the obas.

**ROYAL OBA HEAD**
Sculptures of the oba's head were made in brass, a shiny reddish metal. The obas liked brass because it was bright, bold, and did not rust.

**Look closely**
This sculpture shows the oba wearing a crown and beaded collar.

## LEOPARD WATER JUG

Bronze leopards were popular in Benin's royal art. Some obas even kept real leopards to show they could tame these fierce animals.

### Look closely

The tail of this bronze leopard was used as a handle. Water was poured from its mouth over the oba's hands to clean them.

## PLAQUES OF THE OBA

A plaque is a flat sheet of metal that shows a picture. Small plaques were placed all around the oba's palace.

### Look closely

The oba's size shows that he was more powerful than the people in his kingdom.

## Activities

1. **DRAW IT** Make a picture of an animal that shows people what you are like. Explain your choice.

2. **CONNECT IT** Write a few sentences about how we honor leaders in the United States today.

 **Visit Education Place for more primary sources.** www.eduplace.com/nycssp/

▶ **WHAT TO KNOW**
What are some cultural traditions in Nigeria?

▶ **VOCABULARY**
**diversity**
**heritage**
**artisan**
**folktale**

◎ **READING SKILL**
**Main Idea and Details**
As you read, list important details about Nigeria's cultural traditions.

# NIGERIA
## People and Culture

Today, more people live in Nigeria than in any other African country. A little more than half the people in Nigeria live in rural areas. The rest live in urban areas.

Like the United States, Nigeria is a country of great diversity. **Diversity** means variety or differences. Nigerians belong to more than 250 ethnic groups. They have different customs, religions, and languages. However, all Nigerians share a national culture.

**Many Nigerians buy and sell goods at open-air markets.**

Largest Groups
in Nigeria

**Skill** **Reading Graphs**
Which group has more
people, the Igbo or
the Hausa?

**Education** These Nigerian
children attend a religious
school where they learn
about their heritage.

## The People of Nigeria

In Lesson 3 you read about the Hausa, Yoruba, and Igbo
ethnic groups. These groups and others still live in Nigeria.
Today, they are all part of one nation. Nigerians have close
ties to their own ethnic groups, as well as to their nation.

Each ethnic group in Nigeria has a common heritage.
**Heritage** is the history, ideas, and beliefs that people receive
from the past. Each group's heritage is different, but they
share some beliefs. Family is an important part of culture
for many Nigerians. Each group believes in keeping their
language and traditions alive.

Nigerians also share their national culture and national
laws. Children go to school and learn English, which is
Nigeria's official language.

✓**READING CHECK** MAIN IDEA AND DETAILS What cultures are
Nigerians a part of?

## Nigeria's Cultural Heritage

Much of Nigeria's rich culture is based on traditions of the past. Like people more than 100 years ago, some Hausa artisans use pits to dye, or color, fabrics. An **artisan** is a skilled worker who makes goods by hand. Nigerians are also still known for their metal sculptures, carved masks, and baskets. Traditional music, dance, storytelling, and sports continue to be important parts of Nigerian life as well.

Nigerians today use arts from the past to create new works of art. Nigerian musicians combine traditional songs and instruments with modern styles. Nigerian writers use ideas and lessons from folktales in stories about life today. A **folktale** is a story passed from one generation to the next.

Nigerians also shape their heritage as they make new traditions. Today, soccer is a very popular sport. It has become a big part of Nigeria's national culture.

✔ **READING CHECK** **GENERALIZE** How have traditions of the past affected Nigeria's culture today?

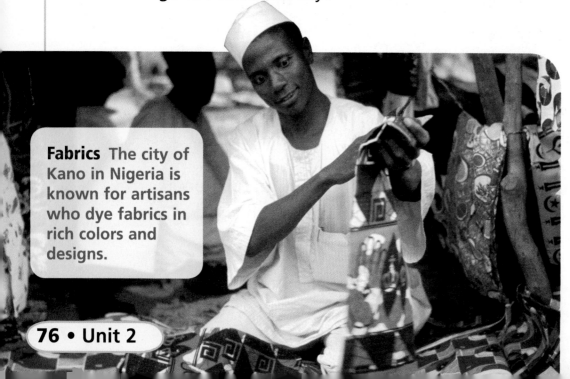

**Fabrics** The city of Kano in Nigeria is known for artisans who dye fabrics in rich colors and designs.

**Music** King Sunny Ade's music is known all over the world. His style of music is called *ju ju*. It combines traditional drums with modern instruments like electric guitars.

**Soccer** Nigerians call soccer football. The Super Falcons are Nigeria's national women's team. They have won the African Championship more times than any other team.

## Religions and Celebrations

Nigerians practice several different religions. Many Hausa people are Muslims. Muslims follow a religion called Islam, which was founded by **Muhammad** (mu HAM ihd). Many Igbo and Yoruba are Christians. Christians follow the teachings of **Jesus**. Some Yoruba still follow traditional beliefs that are thousands of years old.

Each religion has its own holidays. Ramadan (ram uh DAHN) is a religious holiday for Muslims. During the holiday, Muslims limit what they eat for one month. Christmas is a Christian holiday. It is celebrated to mark the birth of Jesus. The Egungun (AY guhn guhn) festival is a Yoruban tradition. During this ceremony, the Yoruba honor their relatives from long ago.

✔ **READING CHECK** GENERALIZE How are holidays important to religions?

**SUMMARY**

Each of Nigeria's many ethnic groups has its own cultural heritage. Nigerians also share their national culture.

These Hausa horn-players are announcing a ceremony that marks the end of the month-long Muslim holiday of Ramadan.

## ❶ What to Know

What are some cultural traditions in Nigeria?

## ❷ Reading Skill Main Idea and Details

Complete the graphic organizer to show the main idea and details.

> Nigeria has many cultural traditions.

## ❸ Case Study Detective 🔍

This artifact was made in Nigeria more than 400 years ago. What instrument did people play at that time?

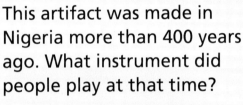

## ❹ Word Play

Use the following clues to figure out the mystery word.

_  O  L  _  T  _  _  E

• passed down from one generation to the next
• a kind of story
• part of many cultures

# Celebrate!

# NIGERIA

**Time to Celebrate!** Nigeria is a country rich in history and culture. People in Nigeria honor their heritage with different celebrations and symbols that express values they are proud of.

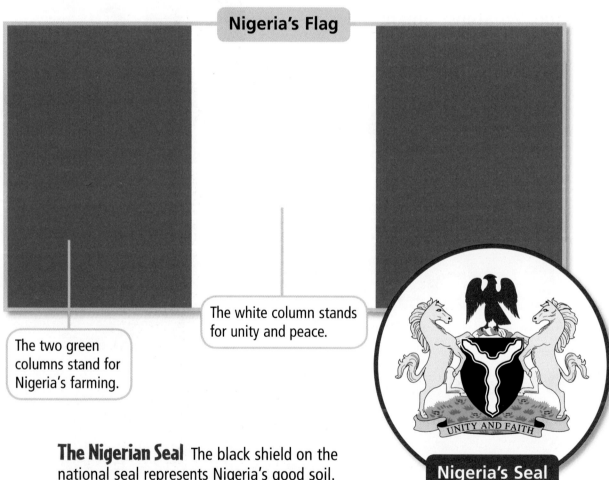

Nigeria's Flag

The white column stands for unity and peace.

The two green columns stand for Nigeria's farming.

Nigeria's Seal

UNITY AND FAITH

**The Nigerian Seal** The black shield on the national seal represents Nigeria's good soil. The silver stripes on the shield stand for the Niger and Benue rivers, which meet to form the country's most important waterway.

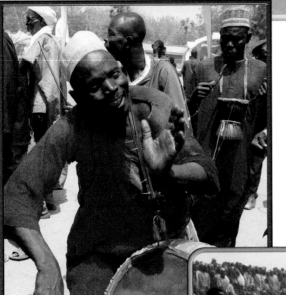

**Fishing Festival** The Argungu (ahr GOON goo) Fishing Festival celebrates the end of many years of fighting between two kingdoms in northwest Nigeria. During this festival, hundreds of people compete to catch the largest fish. The festival also has music, dancing, contests, and shows.

**Yoruban Festival** The Osun Oshogbo (OH soon oh SHOHG boh) festival takes place in the Yoruban city of Oshogbo. The people in this city play music, dance, and feast to honor Osun, one of the goddesses of the Yoruban people.

> **?** How do Nigeria's festivals and symbols show what is important to the people of Nigeria?

# Wole Soyinka

**Why does lightning strike?** In the traditional Yoruba religion, lightning strikes when a god named Shango (shohn GO) throws stones. Wole Soyinka (WOH lay shoy IHNG kuh) writes plays and stories about Yoruba gods such as Shango. Many of his stories are based on Yoruba folktales.

As a boy in Nigeria, Soyinka grew up in the Yoruba culture. Later, he went to England to study. When he returned to Nigeria, he started writing novels, plays, and poetry. He combined African and European traditions.

Soyinka wrote about fairness and difficult choices people had to make. Sometimes government leaders disagreed with what he wrote. He was even put in prison because of his writing. In 1986, Soyinka won the Nobel Prize for his writing. Today, he continues to work for democracy.

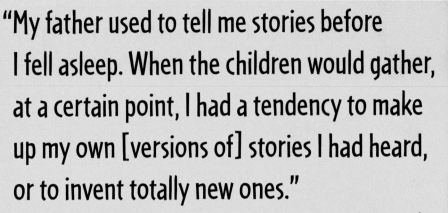

"My father used to tell me stories before I fell asleep. When the children would gather, at a certain point, I had a tendency to make up my own [versions of] stories I had heard, or to invent totally new ones."

–Wole Soyinka

Soyinka (above) gives a speech in Alexandria, Egypt. An actor (left) performs a scene from one of Soyinka's plays in Lagos, Nigeria.

## Activities

1. **TALK ABOUT IT** How did Wole Soyinka show courage as a writer?

2. **WRITE ABOUT IT** Write a story that tells about a choice someone must make. Share your story with a friend.

# Fun with Social Studies

## Postcard Mania

| | 1 | 2 | 3 | 4 | 5 |
|---|---|---|---|---|---|
| **A** | a | b | c | d | e |
| **B** | f | g | h | i | j |
| **C** | k | l | m | n | o |
| **D** | p | q | r | s | t |
| **E** | u | v | w | x | y |

Use the grid to find the missing words in the postcards. Then decide which kind of region each person is visiting in Africa—desert, savanna, or rain forest.

Hi All!
We're here!
We are in the [D-4, A-1, B-3, A-1, D-3, A-1]. It is located in North Africa. This region is very sandy, and the climate is [A-4, D-3, E-5]. However, this region also has the world's longest river, the [C-4, B-4, C-2, A-5]!
Your buddy,
Josh

Dear Grace,
We're here!
This region of Africa is very flat and is covered with tall [B-2, D-3, A-1, D-4, D-4] and few [D-5, D-3, A-5, A-5, D-4]. There are many animals here. We have seen lions, zebras, and [A-5, C-2, A-5, D-1, B-3, A-1, C-4, D-5, D-4]! This place is fun!
Bye for now,
Stacie

Dear Grandpa Joe,
We're here!
It is very [D-3, A-1, B-4, C-4, E-5] in this part of Africa! This region has many kinds of [D-1, C-2, A-1, C-4, D-5, D-4] and animals. We have seen chimpanzees. We also learned about the mountain gorilla, which is [A-5, C-4, A-4, A-1, C-4, B-2, A-5, D-3, A-5, A-4].
Love,
Terry

# Fill It In

VOCABULARY

What's the word? Add the missing letters.

## Clues

1. a waterway made by people
2. a system in which people have no freedom and are forced to work without pay
3. having to do with a city
4. an area under another country's control
5. variety or differences
6. a skilled worker who makes goods by hand

## Words

1. _ _ n a l
2. _ l _ _ e r y
3. u _ b a _
4. c _ _ o n _
5. _ _ v e r _ i t y
6. a _ t i _ a _

 **Go Digital**

# Education Place®
## www.eduplace.com

## Visit Eduplace!

World Communities Now and Long Ago

eGlossary
eWord Game
Biographies
Primary Sources
Write Site
Interactive Maps
GeoGlossary
GeoNet
Online Atlas

Log on to Eduplace to explore Social Studies online. Solve puzzles to watch the skateboarding tricks in eWord Game. Join Chester in GeoNet to see if you can earn enough points to become a GeoChampion, or just play Wacky Web Tales to see how silly your stories can get. Play now at **www.eduplace.com/nycssp/**

# Review for Understanding

## Reading Social Studies

When we **compare** two things, we tell how they are alike. When we **contrast** them, we tell how they are different.

 **Compare and Contrast**

1. Complete this graphic organizer to compare and contrast urban and rural areas in Nigeria today.

**Urban Areas**  **Both**  **Rural Areas**

People live in small villages and grow their own food.

 **Write About the Big Idea**

2. **Write a Paragraph** Culture, history, geography, people, and government all affect Africa's communities. Write a paragraph explaining how government in Nigeria has changed over time.

| | | | | |
|---|---|---|---|---|
| Beginning 500 B.C.E. **The Nok live in northern Nigeria.** | | Beginning C.E. 1000 **The Yoruba create the city of Ife.** | Beginning C.E. 1400 **The kingdom of Benin develops in southern Nigeria.** | C.E. 1472 **European sailors reach Nigeria.** |

500 B.C.E. — B.C.E. | C.E. — C.E. 500 — C.E. 1000 — C.E. 1500

## Vocabulary and Main Ideas

Write a sentence to answer each question.

3. What would you see if you were on a **savanna**?

4. How are resources used for **manufacturing** in Nigeria?

5. What can we learn about the people of Nigeria long ago by looking at **artifacts**?

6. What do **artisans** in Nigeria create?

## Critical Thinking

Write a short answer for each question. Use details to support your answer.

7. Summarize In what ways is Nigeria's government similar to the United States' government?

8. Draw Conclusions Describe the ways in which artisans contribute to Nigeria's cultural heritage.

## Apply Skills

Use the history timeline above to answer each question.

9. How many years are shown on the timeline?

   A. 500 years

   B. 1,000 years

   C. 1,500 years

   D. 2,000 years

10. In what year did European sailors reach Nigeria?

   A. 500 B.C.E.

   B. C.E. 1000

   C. C.E. 1400

   D. C.E. 1472

11. Which of the following dates is the earliest?

   A. 1 B.C.E.

   B. 500 B.C.E.

   C. C.E. 500

   D. C.E. 1000

# Unit 2 Activities

 ## Unit Writing Activity

**Write a Postcard** Write a postcard about a place in Nigeria that you would like to visit.

- Draw a picture of the place on one side of your postcard.
- Write about things you might see in that place on the other side of your postcard.

 ## Unit Project

**Resource Booklet** Create a booklet of Africa's important natural resources.

- List four natural resources found in Africa.
- Tell where in Africa each resource is found.
- Explain how each natural resource is used.

## Read More

- *A Is for Africa* by Ifeoma Onyefulu. Puffin, 1997.
- *A Ticket to Kenya* by Sean McCollum. Carolrhoda Books, 1999.
- *National Geographic Countries of the World: Nigeria* by Bridget Giles. National Geographic Children's Books, 2007.

 visit www.eduplace.com/nycssp/

# Asia

Great Wall, China

## The Big Idea

How do culture, history, geography, people, and government affect communities in Asia?

### WHAT TO KNOW

✓ What are some of Asia's geographic features?

✓ How do people in China use natural resources?

✓ What were some key events in the history of China?

✓ What are some traditions of Chinese culture?

# Almanac

ARCTIC OCEAN

East
Siberian
Sea

Laptev Sea

Kara Sea

Lena River

EUROPE

R U S S I A

Ob River

Ob River

Lena River

Lake
Baikal

Black
Sea

KAZAKHSTAN

MONGOLIA

TURKEY

GEORGIA

ARMENIA

Caspian Sea

Aral
Sea

Lake
Balkhash

CYPRUS

AZERBAIJAN

UZBEKISTAN

Huang He

LEBANON

SYRIA

TURKMENISTAN

KYRGYZSTAN

CHINA

ISRAEL

IRAQ

TAJIKISTAN

JORDAN

IRAN

AFGHANISTAN

Mekong R.

Chang Jiang
(Yangtze R.)

KUWAIT

SAUDI
ARABIA

Persian Gulf

PAKISTAN

Indus R.

Ganges R.

NEPAL

BHUTAN

VIETNAM

BAHRAIN

QATAR

U.A.E.

BANGLADESH

Red Sea

OMAN

MYANMAR
(BURMA)

LAOS

YEMEN

Arabian
Sea

INDIA

THAILAND

Gulf of Aden

Bay of
Bengal

AFRICA

CAMBODIA

INDIAN OCEAN

MALAYSIA

MALDIVES

SRI
LANKA

N

W      E

S

SINGAPORE

Java
Sea

A family in Inner Mongolia, China

Sakhalin

Kuril Islands

PACIFIC OCEAN

A family in India

East China Sea

Ryukyu Islands (Japan)

Philippine Sea

TAIWAN

South China Sea

A family in Vietnam

BRUNEI

INDONESIA

Celebes Sea

EAST TIMOR

## Connect to

# The World

## Asian Countries with the Most People

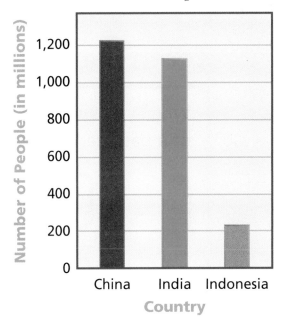

## Asia's Internet Users, 2005

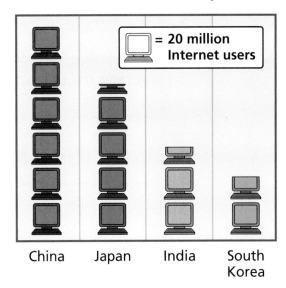

= 20 million Internet users

What do the two graphs tell about China? Which country has more Internet users, India or Japan?

# Reading Social Studies
## ◎ Summarize

**Why It Matters** Summarizing helps you say in a few sentences what is most important in a selection.

## Learn the Skill

When you **summarize**, you retell the main ideas and details of a passage in your own words.

- A summary includes only the main ideas and the most important details, or key facts.
- You can often summarize a paragraph or even a whole selection in just one sentence.

## Practice the Skill

**Read the paragraph. Then summarize it in one sentence.**

**Key Fact** Earthquakes occur when rock deep below Earth's surface moves. This causes the ground to shake. Shaking can be gentle or violent. It usually lasts less than a minute. **Key Fact** Big earthquakes can cause great damage. A big earthquake is often followed by many smaller earthquakes.

## Apply the Skill

# Earthquakes and Volcanoes in Asia

Regions that have earthquakes also have volcanoes. Both volcanoes and earthquakes are caused by movement of rock deep inside Earth. Asia has some of the largest earthquakes and most active volcanoes in the world. Both have caused great damage, near and far.

In 1991, Mount Pinatubo, a volcano in the Philippines, erupted. That eruption sent huge amounts of dust into the air. The dust dimmed sunlight and affected weather all over the world for about a year. In 2004, an earthquake in Indonesia caused huge tidal waves. One wave traveled thousands of miles across the Indian Ocean and hit the coast of Africa.

Many earthquakes occur along a line that runs across Central Asia. Much of China is in this earthquake zone. In 2008, an earthquake in Sichuan (SICH wahn), China, destroyed cities and villages. It caused thousands of deaths. Millions of people were left homeless.

Most of Eastern Asia is part of the Ring of Fire. The Ring of Fire is the name given to the large number of volcanoes that circle the Pacific Ocean. The Ring of Fire runs along the eastern edge of Asia. It is another reminder that Asia is affected by what happens deep inside Earth.

## Summarize

1. How would you summarize the selection?

2. What key facts helped you summarize the selection?

3. What are some details that are not key facts?

# Vocabulary Preview

## peninsula

South Korea is on one of Asia's **peninsulas.** A peninsula is surrounded by water on three sides. **page 99**

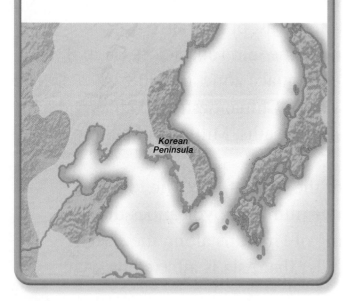

*Korean Peninsula*

## export

Factories in China make toys, shoes, and clothes. These **exports** are shipped to, and sold in, other countries. **page 108**

# Reading Strategy

**Monitor and Clarify** Use the Monitor and Clarify strategy in Lessons 1 and 2.

**Predict and Infer** Use the Predict and Infer strategy in Lessons 3 and 4.

## dynasty

Many generations of the same family ruled China during the Ming **dynasty.** This dynasty lasted almost 300 years. **page 112**

## calligraphy

**Calligraphy** is still practiced in China today. In Chinese calligraphy, artists write characters, or symbols for words, with a brush and ink. **page 124**

**Go Digital** visit www.eduplace.com/nycssp/

# Study Skills

## USE A K-W-L CHART

A K-W-L chart helps you identify what you know and what you want to learn.

- Use the *K* column to list what you know about a topic.

- Use the *W* column to list what you want to know.

- Use the *L* column to list what you learned after reading.

### Asia

| What I Know | What I Want to Know | What I Learned |
|---|---|---|
| Asia is one of Earth's seven continents. | What is the geography of Asia like? | _____ _____ _____ |
| China and Japan are countries in Asia. | What are some other countries in Asia? | _____ _____ _____ |

# This Is Asia

**Before You Read** What was the hottest day, the deepest snow, or heaviest rain you can remember? Think of any kind of weather. You would find it somewhere in Asia.

## The Largest Continent

Asia is the largest continent on Earth. It also has the most people of any continent. More than half the world's people live there. Asia has nearly 50 countries. Two of those countries—China and India—have more people than any other countries in the world.

Most people in Asia live near the coasts or on the thousands of islands of the Pacific and Indian oceans. Many now live in huge cities such as Tokyo, Japan, or Mumbai, India. Others live on farmland, plateaus, tundra, or various landforms of this enormous continent. **Tundra** is a cold, treeless land area.

**Tokyo, Japan** More than 12 million people live in the city of Tokyo.

**Tundra in Russia** Few people live on Asia's tundra.

97

## Regions and Landforms

Asia shares a very large area of land with another continent, Europe. These continents are partly separated by the Ural Mountains. Asia alone includes a third of all the land on Earth. To study such a large continent, geographers have divided Asia into six regions.

Each region of Asia has different landforms and features. East Asia, near the Pacific Ocean, has islands, plains, and plateaus. It also has steep and rugged mountains. Central Asia contains the Gobi Desert, high plateaus, and steppes. A **steppe** is a large grassy plain. The Himalayas, the highest mountain range on Earth, are in this region. North Asia has tundra and part of the largest evergreen forest in the world.

Three regions touch the warm Indian Ocean. Southeast Asia, which includes several large islands, has plains, mountains, and rain forests. South Asia has snowy mountains, plateaus, and sunny seashores. Southwest Asia has the Caucasus (KAW kuh suhs) Mountains and two of the largest deserts in the world.

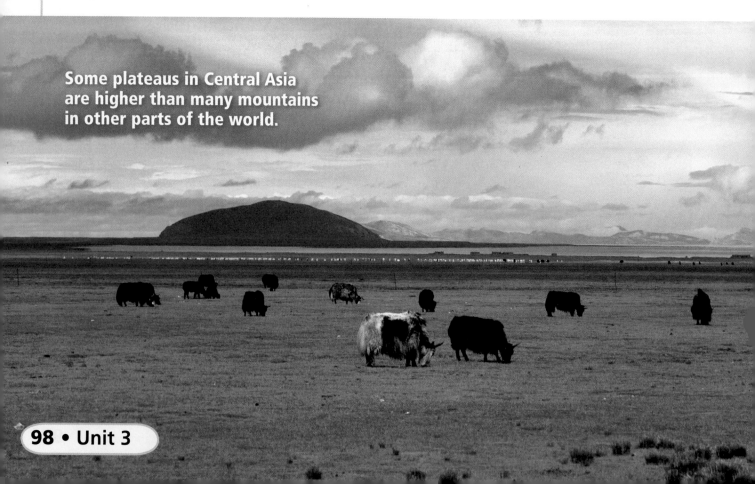

Some plateaus in Central Asia are higher than many mountains in other parts of the world.

## Asia's Landforms

**KEY**

| | |
|---|---|
| | Mountains |
| | Hills |
| | Plateaus |
| | Plains |
| ▲ | Highest point |
| ▲ | Volcano |

## Islands and Water

Asia's rivers supply water to homes, farms, and factories. They are also important for transporting goods and people. Two of Asia's major rivers are the Ganges (GAN jeez) and the Yangtze (YANG tsuh), which is also called the Chang Jiang (chahng jyahng).

Asia is a continent with many seas, islands, and peninsulas. A **peninsula** is land nearly surrounded by water. Four major peninsulas are named on the map of Asia. Japan and some countries in Southeast Asia are archipelagoes. An **archipelago** is a large group of islands. Many of Asia's archipelagoes have active volcanoes.

 **READING CHECK** SUMMARIZE What is Asia's geography like?

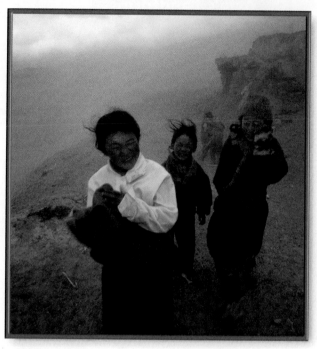

**Monsoons** In some regions of Asia, people expect monsoons during certain months each year.

**Dust Storms** Strong winds sweep across Asia's deserts and plateaus, churning up sand or dust.

# Climate and Natural Resources

Asia's regions have different climates. North Asia has a polar climate, which is cold all year. Central Asia, which is far from the sea, is especially dry and can be very windy.

Winds affect the climates of other regions. Parts of South Asia and the islands of Southeast Asia are sometimes flooded during monsoons. A **monsoon** is a strong wind that brings heavy rain at certain seasons. Southeast Asia's climate is mostly tropical, or warm year round. East Asia has both mild and cool climates.

Besides its great range of climates, Asia has many natural resources. Two major resources are lumber and oil. Mineral resources include silver, gold, iron, and copper. Soil and water are key resources that allow crops, such as rice, to grow. People also use water as a resource for electric power by building dams, such as the Three Gorges Dam in China.

main
(★)
idea

## Plants and Animals

Within Asia's different regions, many varieties of plants grow. They include mosses on the tundra, grasses on the steppes, and bright flowers in tropical regions. Tall, strong trees grow in the rain forests of Southeast Asia.

Some animals depend on certain kinds of plants. Orangutans need forests because they live in treetops. Tigers and elephants need forests or grasslands. As people have built up the land, they have destroyed these animals' homes. The animals are now endangered.

**✓ READING CHECK** COMPARE AND CONTRAST Contrast the climates of Central Asia and Southeast Asia.

**China's giant pandas depend on bamboo forests for their food.**

**SUMMARY**

Asia is the largest continent. Its six different regions feature diverse landforms and bodies of water. Asia has many different climates, natural resources, plants, and animals.

## Lesson Review

**1 WHAT TO KNOW** What are some of Asia's geographic features?

**2 VOCABULARY** Use **archipelago** in a sentence about Asia's landforms.

**3 CRITICAL THINKING: Draw Conclusions** Why are rivers such as the Ganges important?

**4 WRITING ACTIVITY** Choose one of Asia's regions. Using information from the lesson and other sources, create a chart that tells about the region's geographic features.

**5 ⟳ READING SKILL Summarize** Complete the graphic organizer to summarize information about Asia's geography.

## Skillbuilder

# Read a Bar Graph

**China is only one of many countries on the continent of Asia. You can use a bar graph to compare the number of countries on each continent.**

▶ **VOCABULARY**

**bar graph**

## Learn the Skill

Using a **bar graph** is a way to compare amounts. The bars show how much there is of something.

**Step 1:** Read the title. It tells what the graph is about.

**Step 2:** The numbers and words at the left side of the graph tell the amounts. On this graph, the number 20 stands for 20 countries. Each small mark stands for two countries.

**Step 3:** Along the bottom of the graph are the names of the continents.

**Step 4:** Look at the top of the bar above *South America*. It stops one mark above 10. That means that South America has 12 countries. How many countries are in Europe?

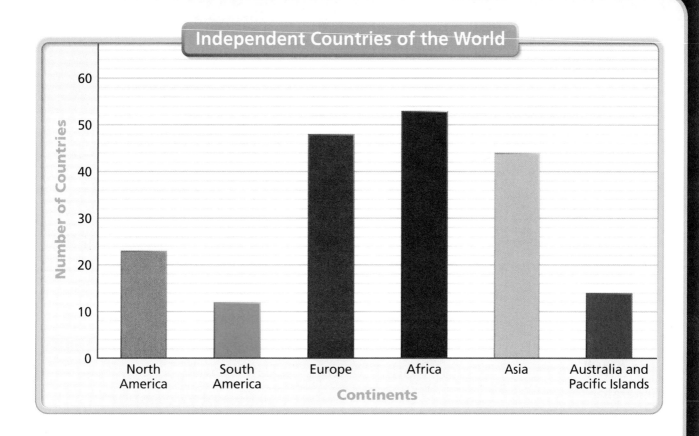

**Independent Countries of the World**

Number of Countries

| Continent | Number |
|---|---|
| North America | 23 |
| South America | 12 |
| Europe | 48 |
| Africa | 53 |
| Asia | 44 |
| Australia and Pacific Islands | 14 |

Continents

## Practice the Skill

Look at the graph above. Then answer the questions.

❶ What is the graph about?

❷ Which continent has the most countries?

❸ Which two continents have fewer countries than North America has?

## Apply the Skill

Turn to page 110 and look at the bar graph of China's top export countries. Which of the three countries shown on the graph buys the most goods from China?

**CASE STUDY**

► **WHAT TO KNOW**
How do people in China use natural resources?

► **VOCABULARY**
irrigation
command economy
export
import

**READING SKILL**
**Generalize** As you read, list facts to help you generalize about China's economy since the late 1970s.

China's economy has grown and changed.

# CHINA
## Land and Economy

*main idea*

China is rich in natural, human, and capital resources. It has the second largest land area of any Asian country. Though China is about the same size as the United States, China has four times as many people. It has more people than any other country in the world.

China has many different geographic features. The Taklimakan and Gobi deserts stretch across the north. Western China has dry plateaus and high mountain ranges. Two rivers, the Chang Jiang and Huang He, begin there. They flow east, through broad plains, toward the Pacific Ocean.

**China's Himalayas have some of the world's highest peaks.**

## Climate and Resources

China's regions have different climates and resources. The high mountains and plateaus in the west have cold winters and hot, dry summers. Farming is difficult there and in the mountainous, dry north. Both regions are rich in mineral resources, such as coal and iron ore.

Most of China's people live in the eastern region, which has many natural resources. It has the sea for fishing and rich soil for farming. Its rivers provide transportation and irrigation. **Irrigation** is bringing water to dry places. The southern part of the region has a subtropical climate, which is mild all year.

✓**READING CHECK** GENERALIZE What generalization can you make about China's resources?

**China's Landforms**

KEY
- Mountains
- Hills
- Plateaus
- Plains
- ▲ Highest point
- —— National border

Heilong River

GOBI DESERT

Taklimakan Desert

CHINA

Huang He

Yellow Sea

PLATEAU OF TIBET

HIMALAYAS

Mount Everest

Chang Jiang (Yangtze R.)

East China Sea

TAIWAN

km 0  200  400
mi 0  200  400

Xi Jiang

PACIFIC OCEAN

Hainan Island

South China Sea

**?** In what direction would you travel to go from the Himalayas to the Taklimakan Desert?

## China's Economy

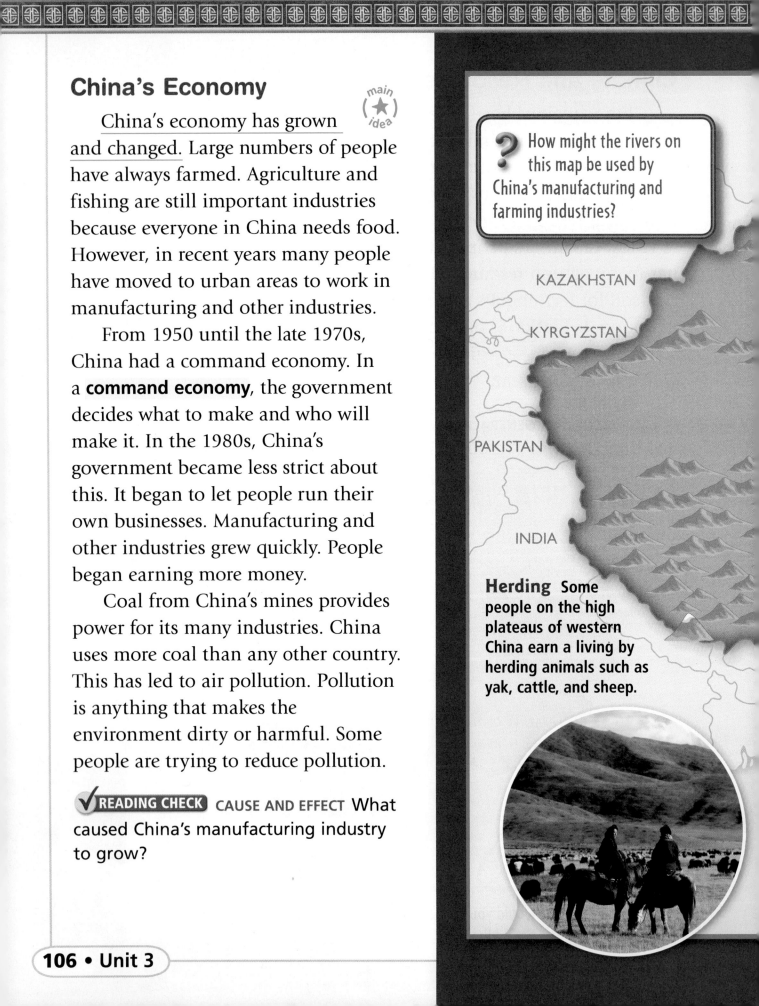

China's economy has grown and changed. Large numbers of people have always farmed. Agriculture and fishing are still important industries because everyone in China needs food. However, in recent years many people have moved to urban areas to work in manufacturing and other industries.

From 1950 until the late 1970s, China had a command economy. In a **command economy**, the government decides what to make and who will make it. In the 1980s, China's government became less strict about this. It began to let people run their own businesses. Manufacturing and other industries grew quickly. People began earning more money.

Coal from China's mines provides power for its many industries. China uses more coal than any other country. This has led to air pollution. Pollution is anything that makes the environment dirty or harmful. Some people are trying to reduce pollution.

✓ **READING CHECK** CAUSE AND EFFECT What caused China's manufacturing industry to grow?

main idea

? How might the rivers on this map be used by China's manufacturing and farming industries?

KAZAKHSTAN

KYRGYZSTAN

PAKISTAN

INDIA

**Herding** Some people on the high plateaus of western China earn a living by herding animals such as yak, cattle, and sheep.

RUSSIA

RUSSIA

Heilong River

MONGOLIA

**Mining** More than half of China's coal and oil are mined in northern and central China. Copper, iron, and other metals are also mined in these regions.

Beijing ★

Huang He

**Manufacturing** Factories in eastern China make many kinds of products, including clothes, televisions, toys, cars, and cell phones.

Shanghai •

• Chengdu

Chang Jiang

INDIA

NP 53

NP 5

NP 5857

km 0    200    400

mi 0    200    400

Guangzhou

Xi Jiang     • Shenzhen

MYANMAR
(BURMA)

N
W    E
S

**Farming** Southern China has most of the country's farmland. Major crops include rice, corn, wheat, fruit, tea, and cotton.

## Manufacturing and Trade

To help its economy grow, China also made changes in trade. Until the late 1970s, it traded with only a few countries. Then China began trading with many more countries. Today, one of China's main trading partners is the United States. The growth of trade has changed where and how Chinese people live. Cities have grown around factories.

main idea

China sells electrical machines, clothing, shoes, toys, and other exports to many countries. An **export** is a good that is shipped and sold to another country. China does not make enough of everything it needs, so it buys some imports, such as chemicals and fuel. An **import** is a good that is bought from another country.

✔ READING CHECK DRAW CONCLUSIONS What does China gain from having both exports and imports?

SUMMARY

China's huge land area has a variety of landforms, climates, and resources. Though the manufacturing industry and trade have grown quickly, farming is still important.

A worker spins thread in one of China's many factories that make cloth.

# CASE STUDY REVIEW

## ❶ What to Know

How do people in China use natural resources?

## ❷ Reading Skill Generalize

Complete the graphic organizer to generalize about this lesson.

China's economy has grown and changed.

## ❸ Case Study Detective

Farmers in China gain space for growing rice by cutting terraces, or steps, into hillsides. How are the two photos of rice farming alike? How are they different?

## ❹ Word Play

Use the following clues to figure out a mystery word about China.

 S  __ B  __ R  O  __ __  C  __ L

- It's a kind of climate.
- It is mild year round.
- China's southeast has it.

# Made in China

**Do you own anything made in China?** The bar graph below shows that China sells more than 200 billion dollars' worth of exports to the United States in a year.

Chinese companies send goods such as electronics, machines, clothing, shoes, toys, and food to the United States. These goods travel far to get to stores in your community.

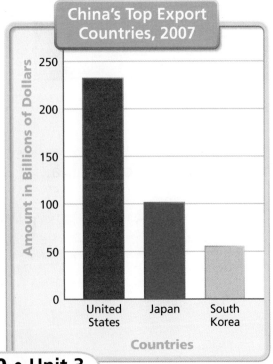

China's Top Export Countries, 2007

Amount in Billions of Dollars

Countries

Follow a bike's path from Wuxi (WOO SHEE), China, to New York City.

Wuxi, China

Zhangjiagang, China

**1**

## From Wuxi to Zhangjiagang

Factory workers in Wuxi make the bike. A truck drives the bike to Zhangjiagang (JAHNG jee yah GAHNG) Harbor. Workers load the bike onto a ship.

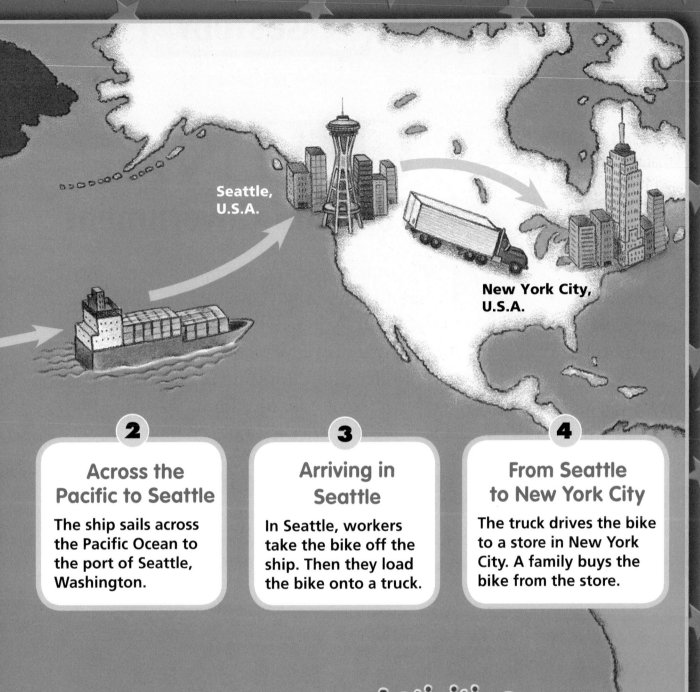

Seattle, U.S.A.

New York City, U.S.A.

PACIFIC OCEAN

### 2 Across the Pacific to Seattle

The ship sails across the Pacific Ocean to the port of Seattle, Washington.

### 3 Arriving in Seattle

In Seattle, workers take the bike off the ship. Then they load the bike onto a truck.

### 4 From Seattle to New York City

The truck drives the bike to a store in New York City. A family buys the bike from the store.

## Activities

1. **TALK ABOUT IT** Of the three countries on the bar graph, which one buys the fewest exports from China?

2. **CHART IT** Read the labels on three different products to find out where they were made. Make a chart that lists each product and the country where it was made.

# CHINA
## History and Government

▶ **WHAT TO KNOW**
What were some key events in the history of China?

▶ **VOCABULARY**

**dynasty**
**compass**
**republic**
**communist**

🎯 **READING SKILL**

**Sequence** Write events in China's history from 1911 to 1979 in the order that they happened.

| 1 | |
|---|---|
| 2 | |
| 3 | |
| 4 | |

Thousands of years ago, people formed small communities in the land we now call China. Almost 4,000 years ago, the Shang dynasty began to rule over some of this land. A **dynasty** is a series of rulers from the same family. China was ruled by different dynasties for more than 3,000 years. Some dynasties did not last long, but others lasted hundreds of years.

In 221 B.C.E., the Qin (CHIN) dynasty united the area's communities into one country. People believe that China's name comes from this dynasty. During the time of dynasties, China became the most powerful country in East Asia.

## Inventions and Achievements

Some dynasties forced thousands of workers to build palaces, bridges, and other structures. The rulers wanted these projects to show off their power. Some projects also improved life for ordinary people. The Great Wall of China was first built during the Qin dynasty. It protected China's northern border and became a safe travel route.

During these years, Chinese people invented tools and products that people still use. One of the earliest inventions was silk, a fine, shiny cloth. Later, the Chinese invented paper. The compass was another invention. A **compass** is a tool used to figure out geographic direction. Other Chinese inventions included printing, porcelain, and gunpowder.

**✓ READING CHECK** SEQUENCE What did the Chinese invent before paper?

Porcelain, a delicate and valuable form of pottery, was first made during the Han dynasty (206 B.C.E.–C.E. 220).

During the Qin dynasty, the Great Wall was created to connect many smaller walls. Later dynasties made the wall even longer.

## Becoming a Republic

In the 1800s, China lost power to countries such as Britain, France, and Japan. Meanwhile, many Chinese people became very poor. Crops failed, and people went hungry. Many Chinese became unhappy with the rule of dynasties. They wanted China to become a republic. A **republic** is a form of government with elected leaders.

Dr. **Sun Yat-sen** (SOON YAHT SEHN), later called "the father of China," led the change to a republic. His group, the Nationalist Party, wanted their nation to be a democracy. In 1911, they took ruling power away from the Qing (ching) dynasty and formed the Chinese Republic. They shared power with another group, the Communist Party, for a while. A **communist** is someone who believes the government should own a country's resources and decide how to divide them among the people.

## China's Leaders

| 1910 | 1925 | 1940 |
|------|------|------|

**1911** Sun Yat-sen leads the Nationalist Party to end the rule of dynasties.

**1935** Chiang Kai-shek, leader of the Nationalist Party, wins control of the government.

## The People's Republic of China

In the 1940s, the Communist Party grew stronger. Its leader, **Mao Zedong** (MOU zuh DOONG), defeated the Nationalist Party leader, **Chiang Kai-shek** (CHANG ky SHECK). Mao turned almost all of China into a communist country called the People's Republic of China. The government took land from its owners and created huge farms where people worked together. People had to do what the government said was best for them. Anyone who disagreed was punished.

Mao died in 1976. Leaders who came after him did things differently. They worked together and listened to others. Some, like **Deng Xiaoping** (DUHNG show PIHNG), moved away from some communist ideas. People could own property and start businesses. China began trading with countries that were not communist.

✔ **READING CHECK** COMPARE AND CONTRAST How were Mao and Sun Yat-sen alike?

1955    1970    1985

**1949** Mao Zedong, leader of the Communist Party, wins control of the government.

**1979** China's President, Deng Xiaoping, opens China to trade with more countries.

## China's Government Today

The People's Republic of China has lasted close to 60 years. During these years, the government of China has changed. <u>To make China a strong, successful country, Communist Party leaders after Mao let go of some communist ideas.</u>

*main idea*

The chart below shows some ways China's government has changed. China is more free than it used to be, but many people want more freedom. The government still punishes people for practicing some religions and for speaking freely.

✓**READING CHECK** CAUSE AND EFFECT What caused China's leaders after Mao to let go of some communist ideas?

**SUMMARY**

Dynasties ruled China for more than 3,000 years. After China became a republic, the Communist Party took control. Communist leaders have made changes over time.

**Skill** **Reading Charts** What is something that people in China could not do in 1955 that they can do now?

### China's Government, Then and Now

| 1955, with Mao Zedong as leader | Today, with current leaders |
| --- | --- |
| • People could not own property | • People can own property |
| • People could vote, but few choices | • People can vote, with more choices |
| • No freedom of religion | • Freedom of some religions |
| • No freedom of speech | • Little freedom of speech |

## ❶ What to Know

What were some key events in the history of China?

## ❷ Reading Skill Sequence

Complete the graphic organizer with
events in China's history from 1911 to 1979.

| 1 | |
|---|---|
| 2 | |
| 3 | |
| 4 | |

## ❸ Case Study Detective

This building is part of the
Forbidden City, which was
built for Chinese rulers
about 600 years ago. At
the time, entering the
building was forbidden
(not allowed) for most
people. How can you tell
that people are no longer
forbidden from visiting?

## ❹ Word Play

Read the meaning and fill in the missing letters in the
middle of each of these words for kinds of government.

- a series of rulers from the same family:
  dy __ __ __ ty
- government with elected leaders:    rep __ __ __ ic
- government that owns all resources:  comm __ __ __ st

# Women Leaders

**One led an army of thousands. The other ruled a kingdom.** Fu Hao (foo how) and Empress Lü (loo) were powerful women who lived when the dynasties ruled China. An empress is a woman ruler.

**Jade Figure**
This figure was found in Fu Hao's tomb. The figure is dressed in the type of clothing people wore during the Shang dynasty.

## Fu Hao

How do we know about someone who lived more than 3,000 years ago? In 1976, Fu Hao's grave was discovered near Anyang (ahn yahng), China. The shells, statues, bones, and pottery found there hold clues about her life.

Fu Hao was married to a king of the Shang dynasty. Scholars believe she led soldiers into battle against nearby states. Once, Fu Hao led an army of 13,000 fighters. To honor her high position, Fu Hao was given her own estate, or land and a big house.

## Empress Lü

Like Fu Hao, Empress Lü had a great deal of power. She was married to the founder of the Han dynasty. In ancient China, only males could rule directly. Empress Lü, however, found a way to take charge when her husband died. She took over the duties of the two infant boys who were in line to become emperor, or ruler.

Ancient stories describe Empress Lü as a leader who showed no pity. She gave important jobs only to her own family members.

Empress Lü ruled for eight years. When she died in 180 B.C.E., her husband's family took back its throne.

**Female Dancer** An artist made this sculpture during the Han dynasty. Compare this sculpture with the jade figure.

## Activities

1. **DRAW IT** Choose one sculpture and make a drawing of it. What do you think the artifact tells about the dynasty?

2. **PRESENT IT** Find out about another leader in China's history. Write two fact cards for a short oral report.

**Skillbuilder**

# Identify Primary and Secondary Sources

▶ **VOCABULARY**

primary source

secondary source

Throughout history, people have written about their lives. Accounts, or stories, such as these are primary sources. A primary source is one created by a person who was there. Primary sources include paintings, photos, and artifacts, as well as writings. A primary source is different from a secondary source. A secondary source is created by a person who was not there.

Read the two descriptions below. One is a primary source and the other is a secondary source.

Ban Zhao (bahn joo) lived between C.E. 45 and C.E. 116. She helped write a history of the Han dynasty. Zhao also wrote "Lessons for Women." In it she gave advice to her daughters about learning the customs of married Chinese women.

James Hunt, 2008

But I do grieve [feel sad] that you, my daughters, just now at the age for marriage . . . have not learned the proper customs for married women. . . . At hours of leisure [free time] I have composed . . . these instructions under the title, "Lessons for Women."

Ban Zhao, C.E. 45–C.E. 116

## Learn the Skill

**Step 1:** Read the sources carefully. What are they about?

**Step 2:** As you read, look for clues that show that the writer lived at the time of the event and was there. The writer of a primary source may use words such as *I*, *me*, or *we*.

**Step 3:** Look for clues that show the writer was not present at the event. If the account is based on what the writer has learned or knows about the event, it is a secondary source.

## Practice the Skill

Answer these questions about the two accounts.

**1** What makes these two accounts different?

**2** Which is the primary source? Explain your answer.

**3** Which is the secondary source? Explain your answer.

## Apply the Skill

Look through Lesson 3 again. List three facts or statements you might find in a secondary source about China's history.

▶ **WHAT TO KNOW**
What are some traditions of Chinese culture?

▶ **VOCABULARY**
elder
ancestor
calligraphy
martial art

**READING SKILL**
**Main Idea and Details**
As you read, find details to support the main idea that traditions are part of life in China today.

Traditions are part of life in China today.

# CHINA
## People and Culture

More people live in China than in any other country in the world. There are more than 1.3 billion people there. That's about 1 billion more than in the United States.

China has more than fifty different ethnic groups. However, most people in China belong to one ethnic group called the Han. The Han share many cultural traditions and the written Chinese language. Most Han can read Chinese characters, or symbols for words. The words may sound different because Chinese has many dialects, or spoken forms of the same language.

Chinese characters stand for words or parts of words. They are different from letters, which stand for sounds, such as in the English alphabet.

## Ideas and Family Life

Since the time of the earliest dynasties, certain ideas have been part of family life in China. One idea is that people should show respect for leaders, teachers, and elders. An **elder** is an older person, such as a grandparent. Another idea is that people should live in peace with nature.

These ideas affected the way people lived long ago. To have nature in their lives, some families built homes around yards with plants and sunlight. To show respect, families had special places in their homes to honor ancestors. An **ancestor** is someone in your family who lived long before you. Grandparents, parents, and children lived and worked together on farms. Family traditions were strong.

Today, many Chinese live in busy cities like Shanghai and Beijing. Their families are smaller, but grandparents still live and help in the home. Urban and rural families still follow some traditional ideas.

✔ **READING CHECK** MAIN IDEA AND DETAILS
What is one way Chinese families today follow traditional ideas of Chinese culture?

Respecting elders and spending time in nature are strong Chinese traditions.

**Painting** This nature scene was painted in 1995 in a style that began hundreds of years ago. The painter also followed the tradition of including calligraphy with the scene.

## China's Traditional Arts

Many arts in China today are based on China's traditional culture. Many painters of nature today respect the ways of painters in dynasties of the past. The art of calligraphy follows early traditions. In China, **calligraphy** is writing characters with brush and ink.

Drama, or acting, is a favorite art form in China. One type of drama called jingxi (jing shi) became popular in the 1800s. The performers act out traditional stories. They follow strict rules for training their voices and bodies.

People also train their bodies when they practice martial arts. **Martial art** is the art of using the body for self-defense. Chinese soldiers in early dynasties learned martial arts. Athletes today use balance, control, and other skills as they practice martial arts such as kung fu.

✔ **READING CHECK** COMPARE AND CONTRAST How are martial arts and jingxi alike?

**Martial Arts** Today, adults and children practice martial arts for health, balance, and fun. In martial arts classes, students show respect for teachers.

**Drama** Performers of jingxi speak, sing, dance, and do acrobatic tricks. The musicians play drums, flutes, and stringed instruments. Some performers now appear in films and on television.

## Going to School

In China today, children start primary school at age six. Students begin the day by saluting China's flag, singing their national anthem, and doing exercises. Then they learn math, history, science, Chinese, English, and other subjects. After school, many do sports or traditional arts.

Students go on to junior high school. At about age 15, they must pass a test and also pay to enter high school. In rural areas, many students stop at that age. In urban areas, more students go on to high school and college.

✓ **READING CHECK** **DRAW CONCLUSIONS** What is one reason students in rural areas might end school at age 15?

**SUMMARY**

Most Chinese are Han, but China has people of many ethnic groups. Chinese traditions and ideas can be seen in family life, in the arts, and in schools today.

**Many classrooms in China's schools have more than 50 students.**

# CASE STUDY REVIEW

## ❶ What to Know

What are some traditions of Chinese culture?

## ❷ Reading Skill  Main Idea and Details

Complete the graphic organizer to show details supporting the main idea.

> Traditions are part of life in China today.
>
> ☐  ☐  ☐

## ❸ Case Study Detective

What are these musicians doing? What can you tell about Chinese traditions from looking at the instruments and at the musicians' clothes?

## ❹ Word Play

Unscramble these words for Chinese art forms.

ilatrma tsra                    ginpaitn

phgralilcay                     inxjig

# CHINA

**Gongxi facai!** In China, the color red can be seen in many symbols and on holidays. It is the main color of China's flag and seal. People wear red during Chinese New Year, the country's most important holiday.

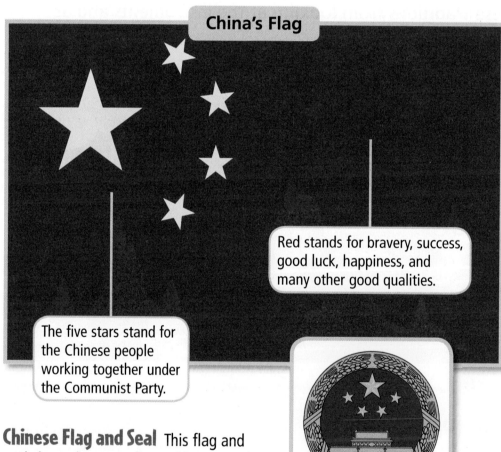

**China's Flag**

Red stands for bravery, success, good luck, happiness, and many other good qualities.

The five stars stand for the Chinese people working together under the Communist Party.

**China's Seal**

**Chinese Flag and Seal** This flag and seal share the same five gold stars and red color. The seal also shows Tiananmen Gate in Beijing. The gate is an important place in China's history.

**Chinese New Year** China's New Year begins in late January or in February and lasts for many days. People often travel to visit their families during this time. They wear red clothes and give gifts wrapped in red paper.

**Dragon Boat Festival** This 2000-year-old festival honors the Chinese poet Qu Yuan (CHOO ywan). The main event is dragon boat racing. Long boats shaped like dragons race each other.

**Lantern Festival** The last day of the New Year celebration is the Lantern Festival. On this night, people decorate paper lanterns and carry them to a parade. Dancers run through the streets, carrying a dragon made of silk, bamboo, and paper.

 In what ways is the color red used in symbols and celebrations of China?

# SAYINGS OF CONFUCIUS

**Treat others the way you want to be treated.** This saying is known as the Golden Rule. Sayings like this are important in many cultures. Confucius (kuhn FYOO shuhs), a great teacher in ancient China, helped people think about how their actions affected others.

Confucius lived more than two thousand years ago. He spent much of his life teaching. He taught ways to show respect in families, schools, and government. After he died, his students collected his sayings into a book called *Lunyu* (LOON YOO). Many of the sayings teach others about caring, respect, and responsibility. The sayings on page 131 are from the book.

In this statue, Confucius wears a long robe. In ancient China only thinkers and teachers wore robes such as this.

# ON CARING

*"What you do not wish for yourself,
do not do to others."*

(Treat others the same way you would treat yourself.)

# ON RESPECT

*"At home, be courteous. At work, respectful."*

(Be polite to your family.
Respect people who work with you.)

# ON RESPONSIBILITY

*"Comfort the aged, be trustworthy
to friends, care for the young."*

(Take care of your family, be honest with your friends,
and help take care of children.)

## Activities

1. **DRAW IT** Choose one of the sayings of Confucius. Draw a picture that shows what it means.

2. **CONNECT IT** Write your own saying about how people can show caring or respect for others.

 **Visit Education Place for more primary sources. www.eduplace.com/nycssp/**

Picture Clues

ahc VOCABULARY

This crossword puzzle is complete, but which picture clues match the puzzle words? One is done for you.

```
                    5.
              1. T R A D E
         4.            R
            E          C
            X          H
      2. P E N I N S U L A
            O          P
            R          E
   3. M A R T I A L A R T
                       L
                       A
                       G
                       O
```

## Across
1.    2.    3.

## Down
4.    5.

# Take One Out

**VOCABULARY**

Each book in the library has a mixed-up word in its title. Fix it.

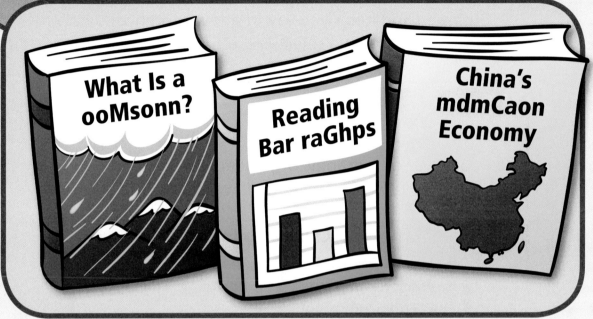

What Is a ooMsonn?

Reading Bar raGhps

China's mdmCaon Economy

**Go Digital**

# Education Place®

www.eduplace.com

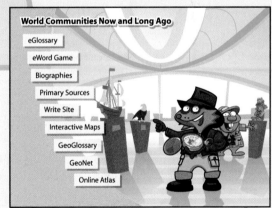

**World Communities Now and Long Ago**

- eGlossary
- eWord Game
- Biographies
- Primary Sources
- Write Site
- Interactive Maps
- GeoGlossary
- GeoNet
- Online Atlas

## Visit Eduplace!

Log on to Eduplace to explore Social Studies online. Solve puzzles to watch the skateboarding tricks in eWord Game. Join Chester in GeoNet to see if you can earn enough points to become a GeoChampion, or just play Wacky Web Tales to see how silly your stories can get. Play now at **www.eduplace.com/nycssp/**

# Review for Understanding

## Reading Social Studies

**Summarizing** helps you say in a few sentences what is most important in a selection.

### Summarize

1. Complete this graphic organizer to show that you can summarize what you've read about China's culture.

**China's Culture**

| Key fact: Respecting elders is an important part of Chinese culture. | Key fact: |
|---|---|

Summary:

## Write About the Big Idea

2. **Write a Paragraph** Culture, history, geography, people, and government all affect communities in Asia. Write a paragraph about how geography affects life in China.

## Vocabulary and Main Ideas

Write a sentence to answer each question.

3. Which countries in Asia are **archipelagoes**?

4. What happened to China's **command economy** in the early 1980s?

5. What were three inventions from the time of China's **dynasties**?

6. How did families in China long ago show respect for **ancestors**?

## Critical Thinking

Write a short answer for each question. Use details to support your answer.

7. **Analyze** In what ways has China's growing economy changed the way people live?

8. **Cause and Effect** How did Mao Zedong's death change China's government?

## Apply Skills

Use the bar graph comparing some of China's largest cities to answer each question.

Large Cities in China

* Counted in 2000

9. Which of the cities on the graph has the most people?

10. About how many people live in Shenzhen?

   A. A little more than 10 million

   B. A little less than 10 million

   C. A little more than 6 million

   D. A little less than 6 million

# Unit 3 Activities

 ## Unit Writing Activity

**Write a Summary** Summarize the information about China's manufacturing and trade on page 108.

- Read the paragraphs and list two or three key facts from each.
- Write a summary that uses the key facts on your list.

 ## Unit Project

**Class Magazine** Create a magazine about different countries in Asia.

- Use an encyclopedia to find four key facts about a country in Asia.
- Write a one-page description of the country and attach pictures.
- Combine your page with other students' pages to create a class magazine.

## Read More

- *Explore Asia* by Bobbie Kalman. Crabtree Publishing Company, 2007.
- *People's Republic of China: Enchantment of the World* by Kim Dramer. Children's Press, 2006.
- *A Primary Source Guide to Pakistan* by Kerri O'Donnell. PowerKids Press, 2003.

 visit www.eduplace.com/nycssp/

# Europe

A Swiss village
in the Alps

The
**Big**
Idea

How do culture, history,
geography, people, and
government shape
communities in Europe?

**WHAT TO KNOW**

✓ What are some of Europe's
geographic features?

✓ How do people in Italy use
natural resources?

✓ What are some key events in
Italy's history?

✓ What are some cultural
traditions in Italy?

Europe Today

ARCTIC OCEAN

Barents Sea

ICELAND

ATLANTIC
OCEAN

Norwegian
Sea

Faroe Islands
(Denmark)

Shetland Islands
(U.K.)

Hebrides
(U.K.)

SCOTLAND

NORTHERN
IRELAND

North
Sea

IRELAND

UNITED
KINGDOM

WALES

ENGLAND

Thames R.

English Channel

NETHERLANDS

BELGIUM
LUXEMBOURG

Seine River

FRANCE

MONACO

PORTUGAL

SPAIN

ANDORRA

Corsica

Balearic Islands

Sardinia

Strait of
Gibraltar

SWEDEN

NORWAY

DENMARK

GERMANY

Rhine R.

SWITZERLAND

LIECHTENSTEIN

SAN
MARINO

ITALY

VATICAN
CITY

Tyrrhenian
Sea

M e d i t e r r a n e a n

Sicily

MALTA

Lake
Vänern

Baltic
Sea

FINLAND

ESTONIA

LATVIA

LITHUANIA

KALININGRAD
(Rus.)

POLAND

CZECH REP.

AUSTRIA

SLOVAKIA

HUNGARY

SLOVENIA

CROATIA

BOSNIA &
HERZEGOVINA

SERBIA

Adriatic Sea

MONTENEGRO

KOSOVO

MACEDONIA

ALBANIA

GREECE

Ionian
Sea

Danube R.

White Sea

RUSSIA

Lake
Onega

Lake
Ladoga

Volga River

Rybinsk
Reservoir

BELARUS

UKRAINE

MOLDOVA

ROMANIA

BULGARIA

Black
Sea

TURKEY

Aegean
Sea

Rhodes

Crete

S e a

AFRICA

KEY

National border

km 0   200   400

mi 0   200   400

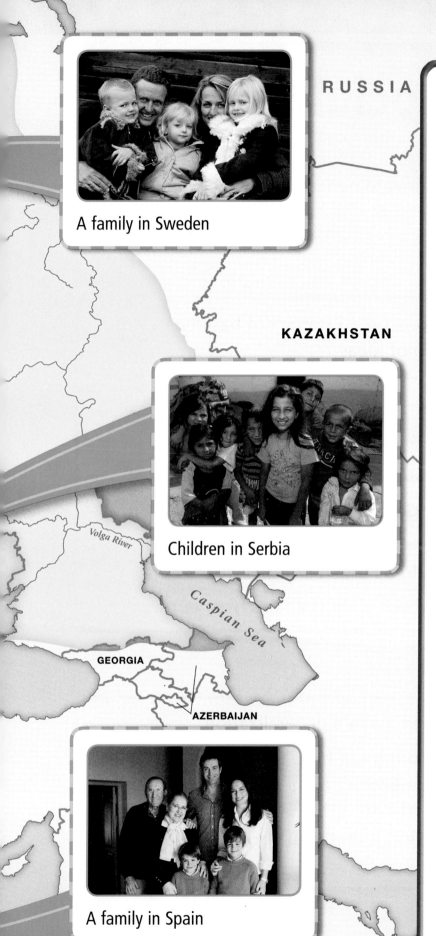

RUSSIA

A family in Sweden

KAZAKHSTAN

Volga River

Children in Serbia

Caspian Sea

GEORGIA

AZERBAIJAN

A family in Spain

# The World

## European Countries with the Most People

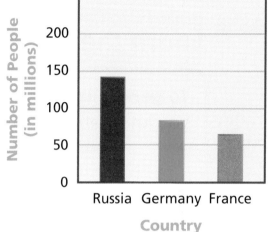

Number of People (in millions)

200
150
100
50
0

Russia Germany France

Country

## Visitors to Europe, 2004

= 10 million tourists

France    Spain    Italy    United Kingdom

- Which European country has the most people?
- Which country had the most visitors in 2004?

# Reading Social Studies

## Generalize

**Why It Matters** Knowing how to generalize can help you understand and remember what you read.

## Learn the Skill

To **generalize** is to make a broad statement based on what you know about a group of ideas.

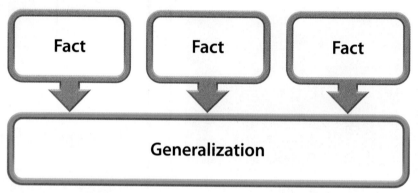

- A generalization should be based on facts.

- To generalize, think about what the facts have in common.

## Practice the Skill

**Read the paragraph. Then make a generalization.**

**Fact**     Rome is a city in the country of Italy. In ancient times, the people of Rome built many roads. Some of the roads were

**Fact** hundreds of miles long. The roads helped the Roman army take over distant lands. Goods and mail also traveled along these roads.

## Apply the Skill

**Read the paragraphs, and answer the questions.**

# Ancient Roman Buildings

Ancient Romans were good builders. Many of the structures they created still exist. The *Pantheon* (PAN thee on) was built in Rome between 118 B.C.E. and C.E. 27. This was a temple, or a place where people performed religious ceremonies. Today, people from around the world visit the *Pantheon*.

Rome once ruled parts of France. In a French town called Orange visitors can see an ancient Roman theater that held 9,000 people. Performers once used the theater for plays, dancing, and juggling.

Between C.E. 110 and C.E. 135, Romans built the Celsus Library in western Turkey. The library held thousands of scrolls, or rolls of paper that people wrote on. The Celsus Library was one of many libraries built by the Romans. Parts of this structure remain today.

## ◎ Generalize

1. What generalization can you make about the selection?

2. The *Pantheon* shows that religion was important to the Romans. Based on the selection, what else do you think was important to them?

# UNIT 4

# Vocabulary Preview

## fjord

The coast of Norway in northern Europe has many **fjords**. These narrow parts of the sea run between cliffs. **page 146**

## empire

Long ago, the city of Rome ruled many nations. Its **empire** stretched over parts of Europe, Africa, and Asia. **page 161**

# Reading Strategy

**Question** Use the question strategy in Lessons 1 and 2.

**Monitor and Clarify** Use the monitor and clarify strategy in Lessons 3 and 4.

## architecture

Ancient Romans created new ways to design buildings. Today, we still use some of the **architecture** they invented.
**page 161**

## festival

At **festivals** held throughout the year, Italians celebrate different parts of their history and culture. **page 172**

Go Digital ▸ visit www.eduplace.com/nycssp/

143

# Study Skills

## USE AN ANTICIPATION GUIDE

An anticipation guide helps you anticipate, or predict, what you will read.

- Look at the lesson titles, section titles, and photos for clues about what you will read.

- Preview the Reading Check questions. Use what you know about the subject to predict the answers.

- Read to find out whether your predictions were correct.

| Europe | | |
|---|---|---|
| **Reading Check** | **Prediction** | **Correct** |
| How does Europe's geography affect its people? | Europe has lots of rivers, which probably make it easy for people to move from place to place. | ✓ |

# This Is Europe

▶ **WHAT TO KNOW**
What are some of Europe's geographic features?

▶ **VOCABULARY**

**fjord**
**coastline**
**moderate**

**READING SKILL**
**Generalize** As you read, list facts about Europe's climate. Then write a generalization based on those facts.

**Before You Read** How long would it take to walk across the United States? Some countries in Europe are so small, you can walk across them in minutes!

## Countries in Europe

Europe has ancient castles and modern skyscrapers. It has tall mountains and low plains. Europe is the second smallest continent, but it has 47 separate countries.

Each country in Europe is different. Each has its own government and culture. The people in each country have their own history and heritage.

Nations in Europe are also alike. They share many landforms and climates. More than half belong to a group called the European Union. These countries team up to make decisions about laws and the economy.

**The European Union**
Leaders of countries in the European Union work together often.

# Europe's Geography

The map on page 147 shows Europe's major landforms. The Alps and the Pyrenees (PEER uh neez) are high mountain ranges in the west. They separate people and countries. The Ural Mountains lie in the east. The Urals separate Europe from the continent of Asia. The Great European Plain stretches from western France to the Ural Mountains. People can move more easily from country to country in this area.

There are thousands of islands off of Europe's coasts. Some of these islands are part of a country in the south called Greece. The mainland of Greece is a peninsula. In the north, the nations of Norway and Sweden also form a peninsula. Fjords (fyawrdz) are found along the coasts of these countries. A **fjord** is a long, deep, narrow part of the sea that cuts into the land and runs between cliffs.

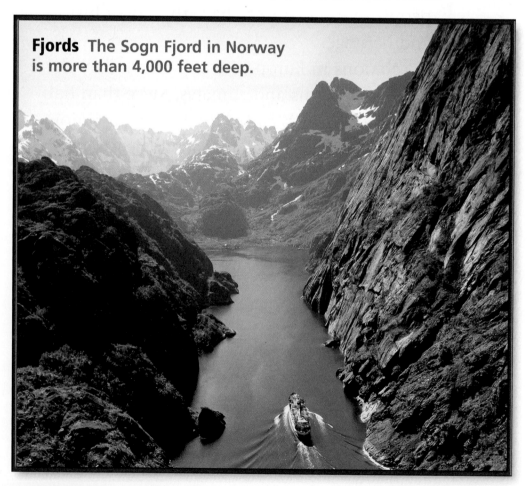

**Fjords** The Sogn Fjord in Norway is more than 4,000 feet deep.

## Europe's Landforms

Barents Sea

URAL MOUNTAINS

Norwegian Sea

KJOLEN MTS.

N
W    E
S

ATLANTIC OCEAN

Lake Saimaa

Lake Onega

Lake Ladoga

EUROPEAN PLAIN

GREAT

Lake Vänern

Lake Peipus

Baltic Sea

Volga River

North Sea

Shannon River

PENNINES

Thames River

Oder River

Elbe R.

Dnieper River

Caspian Sea

Rhine River

CARPATHIAN MTS.

Seine R.

Loire R.

Danube River

Mt. Elbrus CAUCASUS MTS.

Black Sea

ALPS

Po River

Rhône R.

Adriatic Sea

APENNINES

BALKAN MTS.

PYRENEES

Arno R.

Corsica

Tiber River

Tagus River

Sardinia    Sicily

Ionian Sea

Strait of Gibraltar

Mediterranean    Crete    Sea

**KEY**
Mountains
Hills
Plains
▲ Highest point

km 0    200    400
mi 0    200    400

Mountains, hills, and plains are spread throughout Europe.

## Oceans, Seas, and Rivers

Europe's land meets the Arctic Ocean, the Atlantic Ocean, and other smaller seas. The continent's coastline is very long because of its many bends, curves, and islands. A **coastline** is the shape or outline of land where it meets the ocean.

Rivers and other waterways in Europe connect regions and countries. The Rhine River links Switzerland, Germany, and the Netherlands. The Seine River runs through many towns in France. The Thames River connects towns in southern England with the big city of London.

main idea

✓**READING CHECK** GENERALIZE How does Europe's geography affect its people?

147

# Climate, Plants, and Animals

Winds, water, and mountains affect climate in Europe. Warm water near Western Europe gives the region a moderate climate. **Moderate** means mild. Farther from the ocean in Eastern Europe, winters are colder and summers are hotter. Southern Europe, near the Mediterranean Sea, has mild, wet winters and warm, dry summers. Mountain regions can have frigid winters and cool summers.

Different plants and animals live in each kind of climate in Europe. In the coldest areas, mosses and low bushes provide food for reindeer. Near the Mediterranean, many pine forests grow. Wolves and foxes make their homes here. Rabbits, hedgehogs, red squirrels, and songbirds live in parts of Europe, too. Wildflowers grow throughout the continent, even high in the Alps.

**Reindeer** These large animals eat plants that grow in Northern Europe's cold climate.

## Natural Resources

Europe has many natural resources. Its thick forests provide timber for building. The seas and Atlantic Ocean supply the continent with fish.

Europe's moderate climate and rich soil allow farmers to grow crops like grapes, olives, and grains. The soil also provides Europe with important minerals, like coal and iron. Iron is used to make steel, the metal in most cars and buildings. On land that is hard to farm, sheep are raised for wool. Europe's many resources have helped to make its economy strong.

**Using Natural Resources**
Power plants in Europe produce energy using natural resources.

✓**READING CHECK** CAUSE AND EFFECT How does climate affect plants in Europe?

### SUMMARY

Europe is a small continent with geography that connects and separates people. It is rich in resources.

## Lesson Review

**1 WHAT TO KNOW** What are some of Europe's geographic features?

**2 VOCABULARY** Use **fjord** in a sentence about European countries in the north.

**3 CRITICAL THINKING: Compare and Contrast** How might life near a river in Europe be different from life near a mountain?

**4 ART ACTIVITY** Make a booklet showing pictures of plants and animals that live in Europe. Write a sentence about each picture.

**5 🍃 GENERALIZE** Complete the graphic organizer to generalize about Europe's climate.

# Choose the Right Source

▶ **VOCABULARY**

reference book
Internet

You just learned about Europe. What if you still have questions? Different sources of information can help you answer your questions.

## Learn the Skill

**Step 1:** Write down your question.

**Step 2:** Look at different sources of information. Which will best answer your question?

- A **reference book** contains facts on different subjects. You might use a reference book, such as an encyclopedia, to get an idea about a topic.

- Use magazines and newspapers to find out about recent events. These sources also have information about many different subjects.

- The **Internet** is a large system of computer networks. It allows people to communicate and find information on almost any subject.

**Step 3:** Choose the kind of source that will best answer your question.

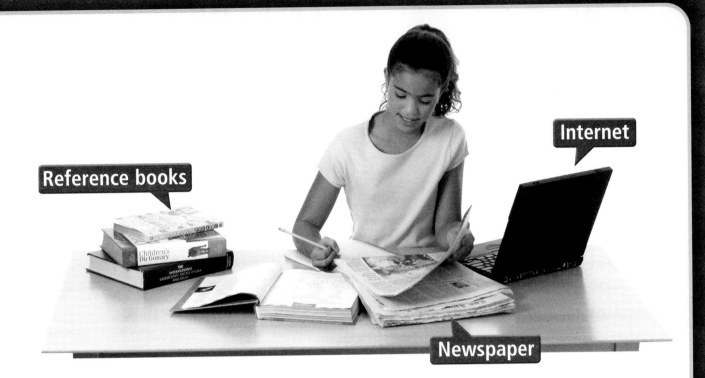

Reference books

Internet

Newspaper

## Practice the Skill

Think about different sources of information. Then answer the questions below.

**1** Which sources of information might you use to find out about Europe's geography?

**2** What sources would you use to find out about local events in European countries?

**3** What would be the best sources of information about the weather in Europe in the last few days?

## Apply the Skill

Think of a question about Europe that you would like to have answered. Then look for the right source to help you answer your question.

# Lesson 2

▶ **WHAT TO KNOW**
How do people in Italy use natural resources?

▶ **VOCABULARY**

producer

market economy

consumer

tourism

**READING SKILL**

**Problem and Solution**
Italy's land is hard to farm. As you read, write down information about how Italy has responded to this problem.

# ITALY
## *Land and Economy*

Italy is a small country in southern Europe. It is shaped like a tall, high-heeled boot. The leg and foot of the boot form a peninsula in the surrounding seas. Two large islands, Sicily and Sardinia, are also part of Italy. Sicily is near Italy's toe. Sardinia is closer to its knee.

Italy's land is mostly high mountains and rolling hills. The Apennine (A puh nyn) Mountains stretch from Italy's toe into the north. Also in the north are the Italian Alps. A large lake called Lake Como lies inside this mountain range. South of the Alps is the Po River Valley, Italy's largest plain.

*main idea*

**Tuscany** This region in northwestern Italy has many hills and valleys.

## Climate and Resources

Northern and southern Italy have different climates. In the south, winters are mild and summers are hot. Places in the north have cold winters and warm summers. In the mountains of both regions, winters are cold. Blizzards can blow through these areas. Even summers here can be cool.

Italy has important resources, including coal, oil, and natural gas. The Po River Valley's soil is good for growing fruits, like strawberries, and the seas around the country are full of fish. Italy lacks many resources, however. Some fuel, foods, and other goods must be bought from other countries.

✔**READING CHECK** **PROBLEM AND SOLUTION** How has Italy solved the problem of not having some important resources?

**Italy's Landforms**

**KEY**
- Mountains
- Hills
- Plains
- ▲ Highest point
- — National border

Mont Blanc
ALPS
Lake Como
Lake Garda
Adige R.
Po River Valley
Po River
APENNINE MOUNTAINS
Arno R.
Adriatic Sea
Ligurian Sea
Tiber R.
ITALY
Volturno R.
Sardinia
Tyrrhenian Sea
Mediterranean Sea
Sicily
Ionian Sea

N W E S

km 0   50   100
mi 0   50   100

? Look at the key. What is land in Sicily like?

## Italy's Economy

Most of Italy's land is hard to farm because of its mountains. Italy's economy is based on service and manufacturing industries rather than farming.

Most Italians work in the service industry. Workers in service jobs do things for others. Bankers, teachers, government officials, and doctors all perform services.

Producers in Italy's manufacturing industry make goods such as machinery, cars, and clothing. A **producer** is someone who makes and sells goods. Italian producers sell many of their goods as exports to other countries.

Italy has a **market economy.** In a market economy, individuals, not the government, decide what jobs they will have. Also, producers decide what to make and what to charge for it. Consumers decide how much of something to buy. A **consumer** is a person who buys or uses a product.

✓ **READING CHECK** **CATEGORIZE** Name three service jobs that people in Italy do.

**Manufacturing**
Most manufacturing in Italy happens in the north. Milan is a major manufacturing center. Factories here produce everything from scooters to books.

? Look at the picture of the gondola driver. What service is he providing the people in the boat?

# Jobs in Italy

AUSTRIA

SLOVENIA

Venice

Florence

Rome

Naples

Bari

**Service Jobs** Venice has many canals. People in Venice sometimes travel in narrow boats called gondolas. Gondola drivers are part of the service industry.

N
W E
S

km 0    50    100

mi 0    50    100

Palermo

**Sicily**

**Farming** Farming is less important than it once was. Some regions still have many farms. Olives are an important crop in southern Italy.

**Fishing** Much of Italy's fish comes from waters around Sicily. The island has three major fishing ports.

## Tourism

One important part of Italy's economy is tourism. **Tourism** is traveling for fun. People who work in the tourism industry provide services to travelers.

Italy welcomes millions of visitors each year. People go to Italy to experience its geography, climate, history, and culture. In Rome, visitors can see ancient buildings and fountains. Museums in Florence show famous paintings and sculptures.

Some tourists are attracted to Italy's geographic features. Skiers and snowboarders travel to the snowy Alps in winter. On the island of Sicily, tourists can visit Mount Etna, an active volcano. People go to the Amalfi Coast for its natural beauty and warm weather.

**✓READING CHECK** MAIN IDEA AND DETAILS List details that support the main idea on this page.

**SUMMARY**

Italy's land is mostly mountains and hills. Farming on this land is hard. Italy has a market economy that depends mostly on manufacturing and services.

Each year, tourists come to Venice for Carnival. People wear costumes and beautiful masks.

Tourists visit the ruins of an ancient building in Sicily.

# CASE STUDY REVIEW

## ❶ What to Know

How do people in Italy use natural resources?

## ❷ Reading Skill  Problem and Solution

Complete the graphic organizer to show the solution to the problem.

Land is hard to farm. ➜ ⬜

## ❸ Case Study Detective

Look carefully at the picture. Have you ever seen a tree like this? Can you guess what kind of fruit these workers are shaking from the tree onto the ground? Hint: The map on pages 154 and 155 has a clue. What industry are these workers part of?

## ❹ Word Play

Try to solve the landform and economy riddles below!

I stretch over Italy, touching its toe and its knee, and on my slopes people like to ski. What am I?

My name begins with a "P" and this is what I do: I make things in factories and then sell them to you. What am I?

# Venice's Grand Canal

**How would you like to take a boat to get to school?** You might have to do that if you lived in Venice, Italy.

Venice is built on more than 100 small islands. Canals crisscross Venice the way that streets cross other cities. People must take ferries, motorboats, and gondolas to get to some parts of the city.

The main waterway in Venice is the Grand Canal. This painting was made by the painter Canaletto almost 300 years ago. It shows the entrance to the Grand Canal. What else do you notice about the painting?

**GONDOLA**

Gondolas are the taxis of Venice.

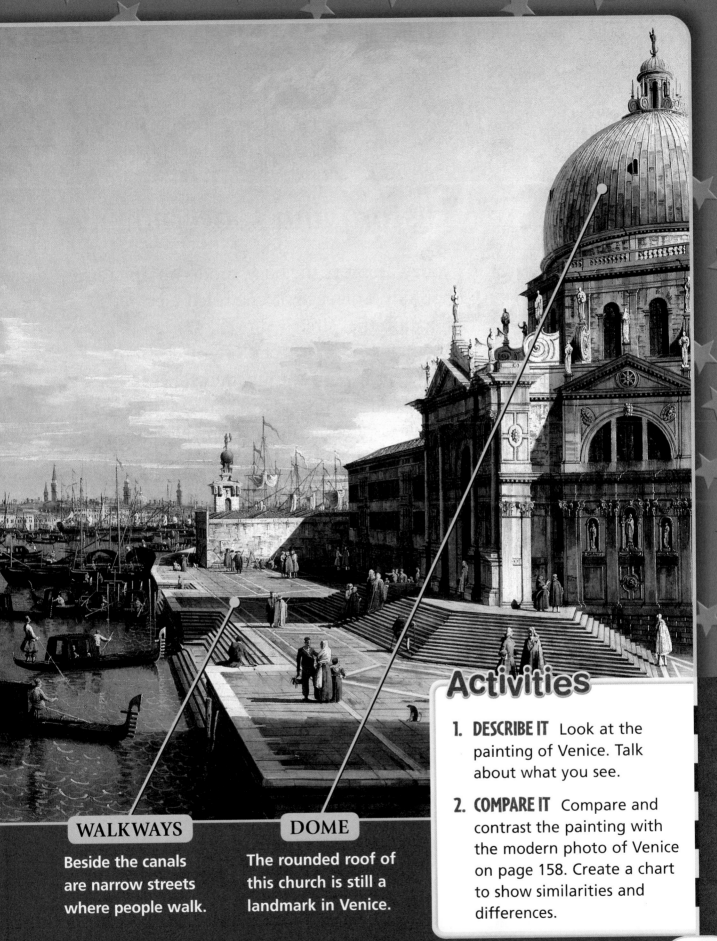

**WALKWAYS**

Beside the canals are narrow streets where people walk.

**DOME**

The rounded roof of this church is still a landmark in Venice.

## Activities

1. **DESCRIBE IT** Look at the painting of Venice. Talk about what you see.

2. **COMPARE IT** Compare and contrast the painting with the modern photo of Venice on page 158. Create a chart to show similarities and differences.

# Lesson 3

**CASE STUDY**

▶ **WHAT TO KNOW**
What are some key events in Italy's history?

▶ **VOCABULARY**

**empire**
**architecture**
**Renaissance**
**constitution**

**READING SKILL**
**Main Idea and Details** As you read, list the main idea and details about Italy's government today.

# ITALY
## History and Government

Today, Rome is the busy, modern, capital city of Italy. Long ago, Rome ruled a powerful civilization that stretched over three continents.

Rome began as a group of villages about 3,000 years ago. Over time, the villages joined together and became a city. At first, kings ruled the city. People became unhappy with these leaders. They overthrew the king and created a republic. In a republic, people vote for leaders to represent them in government. Rome's republic later became one model for the government of the United States.

**The Colosseum**
This stadium was built almost 2,000 years ago in Rome.

## The Roman Empire

Rome's republic had a strong army. Roman soldiers conquered nearby and distant lands. They conquered so many other lands that Rome became an empire. An **empire** is a group of nations ruled by one government. The Roman Empire included parts of Europe, Asia, and Africa.

The Romans had many achievements in government, culture, and architecture. **Architecture** is the design of buildings and other structures. For example, Romans built the Colosseum, a stadium that held about 50,000 people. The Romans also built many roads to connect the distant parts of the empire.

The Roman Empire lasted about 500 years, but then broke apart. It had grown too large for its rulers to control. However, ancient Rome still affects the world with its ideas about government, architecture, and more.

✔ **READING CHECK** MAIN IDEA AND DETAILS What were some of the Romans' achievements?

### Roman Empire

ATLANTIC OCEAN

Corsica

Rome

ITALY

Sardinia

Adriatic Sea

GREECE

Sicily

Black Sea

Caspian Sea

M e d i t e r r a n e a n   S e a

**KEY**

Roman Empire, C.E. 117

km 0   400   800
mi 0   400   800

A F R I C A

EGYPT

Red Sea

? Look at the map and compass rose. Where in the empire is Egypt?

## The Renaissance

After the Roman Empire ended, government on the Italian peninsula changed. There was no longer a single ruler. Instead, Italian cities formed their own governments and became separate countries called city-states.

Many leaders of the Italian city-states thought art was important. In the 1300s, they paid painters, sculptors, architects, and weavers to create works of art. This led to a period called the Renaissance. The **Renaissance** was a time of major change in art and science across Europe. Artists began making their paintings more like real life than before. Scientists made discoveries about medicine and planets. The Renaissance lasted about 300 years.

## Italy's History

1860                  1910

**1860 Garibaldi**
Garibaldi's army defeats two important Italian states and puts them under the control of a king.

**1861 The Kingdom of Italy** Italy becomes a kingdom under this flag.

## Italy's Growth

After the Renaissance, Italy remained divided into small states. In the 1800s, a man named Giuseppe Garibaldi led an army in the fight to bring these states together. By 1861, most of Italy was united under a king.

In the mid-1900s, World War II broke out. Many countries fought in this war, including Italy. Italy was on the side that lost. After the war, Italians had to rebuild parts of the country that were destroyed by fighting. They also voted to change their government to a republic. Italy is still a republic. It is also a member of the European Union. The countries that belong to the European Union work together on many issues. Some of them use the same form of money, the euro, to make trade easier.

✓**READING CHECK** SEQUENCE **Name in order the kinds of government that Italy had after the Roman Empire.**

1960   2010

**1946 Republic**
Italians vote to become a republic. Enrico de Nicola (left) is Italy's first president.

**2002 The Euro**
Italy and other nations in the European Union all agree to use the same money, the euro.

163

## Italy's Government Today

Like many other countries, Italy has a constitution. A **constitution** is a written plan for a country's government.

The Italian constitution divides Italy's government into three branches, or parts. One branch makes laws for the entire country. Another branch makes sure that those laws are obeyed. Italy's president and prime minister are the leaders of that branch. The third branch is made up of judges. They decide whether laws follow the rules of Italy's constitution.

Recently, Italy's government has faced challenges. Some leaders committed crimes while they were part of the government. Italy is working to improve its leadership.

✓ **READING CHECK** GENERALIZE Why is a constitution important?

**SUMMARY**

The Roman Empire spread over parts of three continents. Later, Italian city-states ruled themselves. Today, Italy is a republic with a president and a prime minister.

### Italy's Leaders

| President | Prime Minister |
|---|---|
| • Chosen by lawmakers | • Chosen by the president, and approved by lawmakers |
| • Commands the army | |
| • Can call for new elections | • Chooses other ministers to help run the government |
| • Term lasts seven years | • Term lasts five years |

# CASE STUDY REVIEW

## ❶ What to Know

What are some key events in Italy's history?

## ❷ Reading Skill  Main Idea and Details

Complete the graphic organizer to show the main idea and details about Italy's government today.

Italy's constitution divides the government into three parts.

## ❸ Case Study Detective

Compare the buildings. The one on the left was built in ancient Rome. The one on the right was built in the 1900s in Washington, D.C. How are they alike? How are they different?

Pantheon

Thomas Jefferson Memorial

## ❹ Word Play

The language of the ancient Romans, Latin, is the source of many English words. Write an English word that comes from each root:

| Latin Root | Meaning | English Word |
|---|---|---|
| dent- | tooth | ? |
| port- | carry | ? |
| liber- | free | ? |

# A Roman House

**How old is your city or town?**
Rome is more than 2,500 years old. In ancient Rome, wealthy families had large homes built around private courtyards. Some of their homes had rooms for dining, bathing, and even shopping.

Bath

**Shops** Wealthy Romans sometimes let their outer rooms be used as shops. On the left, a merchant sells pillows and coverings for furniture.

**Dining Room** In this room a wealthy Roman family might eat from dishes made of silver and gold. They would pour beverages from glass jugs like this one.

Courtyard

Front doors

# Activities

1. **EXPLORE IT** Step into the picture. Talk about what it might have been like to live there.

2. **WRITE ABOUT IT** Write a story that takes place in a Roman house. Who are the characters and what happens to them?

## Skillbuilder

# Resolve Conflicts

People in Italy and other nations in Europe often work together on issues such as protecting the environment. Sometimes, though, people have very different ideas. When people do not agree on something, they face a conflict. Listening to others can help them solve their conflicts.

## Learn the Skill

**Step 1:** Identify a conflict. For example, students may have different ideas on how to use a class free period.

**Step 2:** Ask people to share their ideas. For example, some students may want the free period for more computer time. Others might want to play outdoors. Listen to all the ideas.

**Step 3:** Brainstorm different solutions. The class might split the time between the soccer field and the computer room. Or, students could take turns doing different activities on different days.

**Step 4:** Agree to one of the solutions. Each side may have to make a compromise. A **compromise** is a plan that everyone agrees on. When people make a compromise, each person gives something up. Work on the plan until everyone agrees with at least part of the solution.

## Practice the Skill

Use the steps in Learn the Skill to answer these questions about solving conflicts.

**1** Why should people share their ideas?

**2** Why is listening important in solving conflicts?

**3** How can you find out if everyone agrees to the solution?

## Apply the Skill

Suppose your school wants to start a litter clean-up program. Different groups have different ideas about what to do. One group wants to make posters reminding students not to litter. Another group wants to buy more trash cans and recycling bins. Write a paragraph about how these two groups could solve the conflict. Remember that they will probably have to reach a compromise.

## Lesson 4

▶ **WHAT TO KNOW**
What are some cultural traditions in Italy?

▶ **VOCABULARY**

**population**
**opera**
**festival**

**READING SKILL**
**Summarize** As you read, list facts you can use to summarize the arts in Italy.

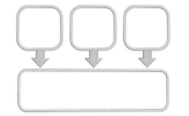

### CASE STUDY

# ITALY
## *People and Culture*

Italy has the fifth largest population in Europe. **Population** is the number of people that live in a place. Almost 60 million people live in Italy. Most live in large cities, especially in northern Italy. In southern Italy there are many smaller cities and villages.

Italy has many different regions with special customs, history, and foods, but Italians all over the country have much in common. Most people in Italy speak the same language, Italian. Most practice the same religion, Roman Catholicism. Italians share many values, including a deep pride in Italian culture.

**Florence, Italy** This northern city is home to almost 400,000 people.

## Families Come First

Families are at the center of most Italians' lives. In cities, families are usually small. Parents and children often live in apartments above shops and restaurants. In rural areas, many families are bigger. Most people live in houses by fields or on hilltops. Children here may share a home with their parents and grandparents.

In all parts of Italy, family gatherings are very important. Meals are one way that families spend time together. Lunch is usually the largest meal of the day, and many people come home to eat with their families. Schools generally let out at one or two o'clock, so children can go home for a family meal.

*main idea* ⭐

In Italy, grandparents, parents, and young children may all live together or close to each other.

✔ **READING CHECK** SUMMARIZE What is life like for people who live in Italian cities?

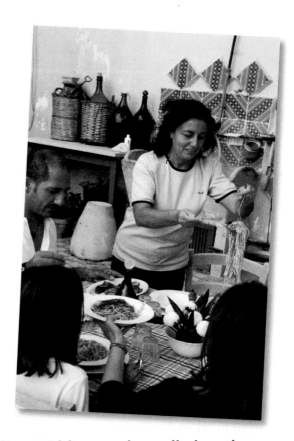

An Italian midday meal usually has three parts: soup or pasta to start, then fish or meat and vegetables, followed by fruit for dessert.

## Italian Culture

Italy has a rich culture. One way Italians enjoy their culture is by going to museums. Some museums have beautiful Italian paintings. Others show food or architecture. In Rome, you can even go to the National Museum of Pasta Foods!

Movies, concerts, and opera are also part of Italian culture. An **opera** is a play in which most words are sung and accompanied by an orchestra. Opera was invented in Italy. So was the piano. Italians are proud of their country's accomplishments in the arts.

Each year, Italy has many festivals. A **festival** is a special event where people celebrate the arts. There are festivals for painting, opera, dance, film, and other Italian art forms.

*main idea*

**✓READING CHECK** GENERALIZE Why do communities hold festivals?

**DANCE** Folk dances are part of Italian culture. They are performed in festivals all over Italy.

**PAINTING** Agnolo Bronzino was an Italian painter during the Renaissance. He painted many portraits of wealthy Italian men and women, such as this woman who lived in the 1500s.

**LITERATURE** Italo Calvino (EE tah loh kahl VEE noh), an Italian writer, wrote down many Italian folktales, as well as modern stories of his own.

Carlo Collodi, another writer, wrote *Pinocchio*, the famous story of a wooden puppet who came to life.

Italo Calvino

173

## Sports in Italy

Italians are enthusiastic sports fans. Italy's number-one sport is soccer, or *calcio* in Italian. In nearly any Italian city on a Sunday afternoon, you will find a stadium filled with fans cheering for their favorite soccer clubs.

Bocce (BOH cheh) is a popular Italian bowling game. It is played outdoors on a long narrow court filled with gravel.

In winter, skiing is a favorite activity. So many Italians take a week's vacation to go skiing that the vacation has a name, *settimana bianca*, or white week.

*main idea*

**✓ READING CHECK** **COMPARE AND CONTRAST** How are sports in Italy similar to and different from sports in the United States?

**SUMMARY**

The people of Italy have much in common. Families are important. Italians love many kinds of arts and sports.

Many Italian families enjoy skiing in the Alps.

# CASE STUDY REVIEW

## ❶ What to Know

What are some cultural traditions in Italy?

## ❷ Reading Skill Summarize

Complete the graphic organizer to summarize what you have read about the arts in Italy.

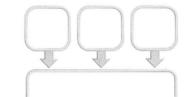

## ❸ Case Study Detective

Look at the photograph. What Italian sport are these men playing? How can you tell?

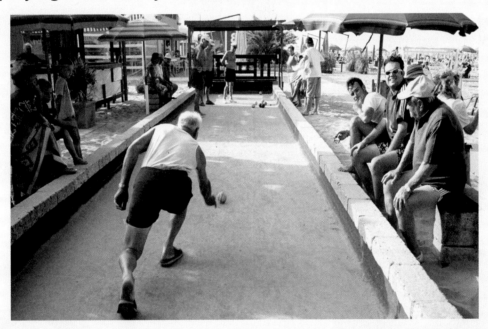

## ❹ Word Play

Unscramble the letters and create words that describe Italian culture.

poaer

satefivl

cobec

eamsl

rsecco

malfiy

# ITALY

**Celebriamo!** In Italy, holidays are times to celebrate. Most people take off work or school to go to parades, festivals, and other events. The country also has national symbols that remind Italians that they are part of one country.

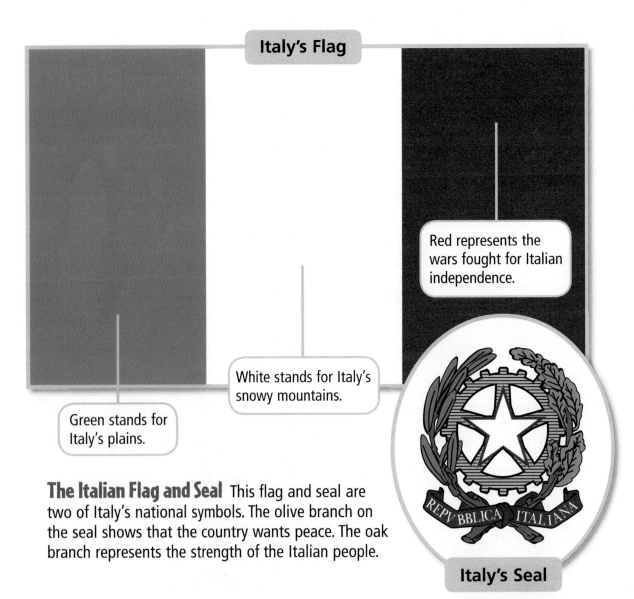

Italy's Flag

Red represents the wars fought for Italian independence.

White stands for Italy's snowy mountains.

Green stands for Italy's plains.

Italy's Seal

REPVBBLICA ITALIANA

**The Italian Flag and Seal** This flag and seal are two of Italy's national symbols. The olive branch on the seal shows that the country wants peace. The oak branch represents the strength of the Italian people.

## Liberation Day (Festa della Liberazione)

In the 1940s, the world was at war and Germany ruled Italy. On April 25, 1945, Italy was liberated, or freed, from German control. Italians celebrate this day with street marches.

## Republic Day (Festa della Repubblica)

This holiday honors the day in 1946 when Italy became a republic after years of kings and other rulers.

**?** How are the two holidays described above like Independence Day in the United States? Explain how the days are similar.

# Biography

# Italian Athletes

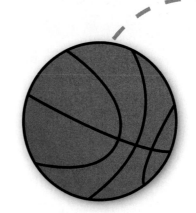

**What sports do you like to play?** In Italy, many people play soccer for fun or for exercise. Italians also participate in other individual and team sports. These sports include skiing, biking, swimming, golf, and basketball. Italians are proud of their athletes. Athletes are people who are very good at a sport. Many of these athletes have played in world competitions such as the Olympics or soccer's World Cup.

## Fabio Cannavaro

As a boy in Naples, Fabio Cannavaro loved playing soccer. When he was 11, Cannavaro joined a junior team for the Napoli Soccer Club. Later, he played for several professional soccer teams in Italy, as well as one in Spain.

Cannavaro played for the Italian team at the 1996 Olympics and in several World Cup tournaments. As captain of Italy's national team, he led his teammates to victory at the 2006 World Cup.

## Andrea Bargnani

Andrea Bargnani joined a professional basketball team in Italy when he was 16. In 2006, he moved from Italy to Canada to join the Toronto Raptors basketball team. He became the fourth Italian player in history to join the National Basketball Association of North America, or the NBA.

Bargnani's nickname, "Il Mago," means "the magician" in Italian. At seven feet tall, he can perform magic on the basketball court!

## Stefania Belmondo

Stefania Belmondo started skiing in Vinadio, Italy when she was only four years old. Skiing was the easiest way to get to school in the snow! Belmondo started racing in cross-country ski events when she was eight. She later became the first Italian woman to win an Olympic medal in skiing.

Belmondo has won ten Olympic medals and many world championships. At the 2006 Olympics in Turin, Italy, Belmondo was selected to light the Olympic torch that burned throughout the games.

## Activities

1. **MAKE IT** Make biography cards for Cannavaro, Belmondo, and Bargnani. List important facts about each athlete on the cards.

2. **WRITE ABOUT IT** Write a story about joining a sports team. Include a problem and solution in your story.

# Fun with Social Studies

## Miss Information

Miss Information is guiding a group of tourists through Italy. Unfortunately, she's sharing a lot of incorrect information. Find the three mistakes.

The Renaissance was a time when there wasn't much growth in art or science in Europe.

Italy's land is mostly flat.

Soccer is a very popular sport in Italy today.

The two islands of Sicily and Sardinia are a part of Italy.

Today, the main language in Italy is German.

Rome's republic was a model for the United States government.

# Alphabet Riddle

Put these words into the grid in alphabetical order. Read down the letters in the green squares to answer the riddle.

coastline
Internet
moderate
empire
population
festival

**Riddle:**

How can you hear a pin drop?

 **Education Place®**
www.eduplace.com

## Visit Eduplace!

Log on to Eduplace to explore Social Studies online. Solve puzzles to watch the skateboarding tricks in eWord Game. Join Chester in GeoNet to see if you can earn enough points to become a GeoChampion, or just play Wacky Web Tales to see how silly your stories can get. Play now at **www.eduplace.com/nycssp/**

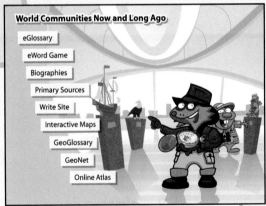

World Communities Now and Long Ago

eGlossary
eWord Game
Biographies
Primary Sources
Write Site
Interactive Maps
GeoGlossary
GeoNet
Online Atlas

## Reading Social Studies

To **generalize** is to collect facts and then make a broad statement based on the facts.

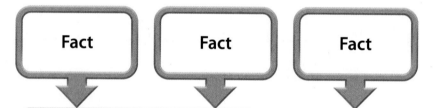

**Generalize**

1. Write facts that support the generalization below about Italian culture.

| Fact | Fact | Fact |
|------|------|------|

**Generalization:**
Sports are an important part of Italian culture.

 **Write About the Big Idea**

2. **Write a Speech** Culture, history, geography, people, and government all affect communities in Europe. Write a speech describing different parts of Italian culture.

## Vocabulary and Main Ideas

**Write a sentence to answer each question.**

3. What is Europe's **coastline** like?

4. In a **market economy**, who decides what is made and how much it costs?

5. Why was the **Renaissance** an important time in Europe's history?

6. Where does most of Italy's **population** live?

## Critical Thinking

**Write a short answer for each question. Use details to support your answer.**

7. **Cause and Effect** How does Italy's lack of good farmland affect what people there do for work?

8. **Compare and Contrast** Compare and contrast the climates of northern and southern Italy.

## Apply Skills

**Resolve Conflicts** Apply what you have learned about resolving conflicts. Read the paragraph below and answer each question.

A group of students have different ideas about how to present their history project. Some of the students want to give a speech. The other students want to make a poster. How should they resolve this conflict?

9. What is the FIRST thing the group should do to resolve the conflict?

10. Which of the following is a compromise?
    - **A.** Make a poster.
    - **B.** Give a speech.
    - **C.** Do separate projects.
    - **D.** Give a speech using a poster.

# Unit 4 Activities

 ## Unit Writing Activity

**Write a Poem** Write a poem about families in Italy.

■ Include details about family meals.

■ Write about sports or other cultural activities that families in Italy might do together.

 ## Unit Project

**Bulletin Board** Create a class bulletin board about interesting places in Europe.

■ Research a place you would like to visit in Europe.

■ Write descriptions and include pictures.

## Read More

■ *Our Amazing Continents: Hello, Europe!* by April Pulley Sayre. Millbrook Press, 2003.

■ *History of the World: The Italian Renaissance* by Don Nardo. KidHaven Press, 2003.

■ *Focus on Sweden* by Nicola Barber. World Almanac Library, 2007.

Go Digital visit www.eduplace.com/nycssp/

# South America

The
**Big**
Idea

How do culture, history, geography, people, and government affect communities in South America?

## WHAT TO KNOW

✓ What are some of South America's geographic features?

✓ How do the people in Brazil use natural resources?

✓ What are some key events in Brazil's history?

✓ What are some cultural traditions in Brazil?

**Ruins of the city of Machu Picchu in the Andes of Peru.**

Caribbean Sea

ATLANTIC OCEAN

Panama Canal

Lake Maracaibo

VENEZUELA

GUYANA

SURINAME

FRENCH GUIANA (Fr.)

COLOMBIA

Galápagos Islands (Ecuador)

ECUADOR

Amazon River

PERU

BRAZIL

PACIFIC OCEAN

Lake Titicaca

BOLIVIA

PARAGUAY

CHILE

Paraná River

URUGUAY

ARGENTINA

Río de la Plata

N
W    E
S

KEY
——— National border

km 0    400    800
mi 0    400    800

Falkland Islands (U.K.)

Strait of Magellan

South Georgia Island (U.K.)

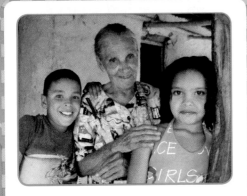

A family from rural Venezuela

A family from the mountains of Peru

ATLANTIC
OCEAN

A family from the city of Buenos Aires, Argentina

## Connect to
# The World

## South American Countries with the Most People

## South American Languages

Most Brazilians speak Portuguese. In almost all other countries most people speak Spanish. South American Indian languages are also spoken.

- Which country has the largest population?
- What is the most widely spoken language in South America?

# Reading Social Studies

## Cause and Effect

**Why It Matters** Understanding cause and effect can help you see why events happen.

## Learn the Skill

A **cause** is something that makes something else happen. An **effect** is the thing that happens as a result of a cause.

- Words and phrases, such as *because*, *as a result*, *since*, and *so,* can help you identify why something happens.

- An effect can also become a cause for another event.

## Practice the Skill

Read the paragraph. Find a cause and an effect.

**Cause**    Every few years, winds that usually blow from east to west over the south Pacific die out or change direction. As a result, **Effect**  warm water flows east from the western Pacific towards South America. The appearance of this warm water off the coast of South America is called *El Niño* (ehl NEE nyoh).

## Apply the Skill

# El Niño

During *El Niño*, the warmer water off the coast of South America warms the air. In this tropical region, warm air causes strong thunderstorms. These storms normally move west. However, during *El Niño*, they move east over South America because they follow the direction of the winds and warm water.

These strong storms cause flooding in areas that don't normally receive large amounts of rainfall. In some of the drier parts of Peru, this increased rainfall can cause floods and mudslides that destroy crops and homes.

The reason why the winds over the Pacific change is unknown, so it is hard to predict when *El Niño* will happen. Scientists are studying better ways to predict *El Niño* because of its serious effects on the weather.

## Cause and Effect

1. Why do strong storms move east instead of west during *El Niño*?

2. Why is it hard to predict when *El Niño* will happen?

3. What effects can the increased rainfall from *El Niño* have on parts of South America?

# Vocabulary Preview

### glacier

The Andes Mountains contain **glaciers.** These huge masses of slow-moving ice do not melt in the summer. **page 194**

### bay

The city of Rio de Janeiro grew around a **bay** on Brazil's Atlantic coast. The bay leads into the Atlantic Ocean. **page 200**

## Reading Strategy

**Summarize** Use the summarize strategy in Lessons 1 and 2.

**Question** Use the question strategy in Lessons 3 and 4.

## modernize

Brazil's leaders have helped to **modernize** their country. In 1960, they started building Brasília, a new capital city for Brazil. **page 210**

## leisure time

Most Brazilians live near the ocean. Many people like to spend their **leisure time** relaxing at a nearby beach. **page 222**

**Go Digital** visit www.eduplace.com/nycssp/

# Study Skills

## WRITE TO LEARN

Write about what you read to better understand and remember information.

- Keep a learning log to write responses to what you read.

- Responses can be personal and creative to make the text more meaningful to you.

### South America

| What I Learned | My Response |
|---|---|
| South America has the world's largest forest and longest mountain chain. | South America has some amazing places to see! |
| The Amazon rain forest is home to many unusual plants and animals. They are protected by the forest's shade. | I would love to see all the different plants and animals that live in the Amazon rain forest! |
| The capybara is the world's largest rodent. It lives in the Amazon rain forest. | Even though a capybara is a rodent, I think it looks more like a pig with fur than a rat. |

# This Is South America

▶ **WHAT TO KNOW**
What are some of South America's geographic features?

▶ **VOCABULARY**
glacier
tributary
strait
elevation

◎ **READING SKILL**
**Cause and Effect** As you read, list South America's main geographic features and their effect on people.

**Before You Read** What is the most unusual geographic feature of your community? If you lived in South America, you would see many amazing landforms and bodies of water.

## Land and People

South America is the fourth largest continent, but it is first in many things. The Amazon rain forest is the world's largest forest. The Andes Mountains are the longest mountain chain. The Amazon River carries more water than any other river.

The continent is divided into twelve countries and a small French territory. Most people in South America have American Indian, European, or African ancestors.

At markets like this one in the Andes, people buy and sell goods.

193

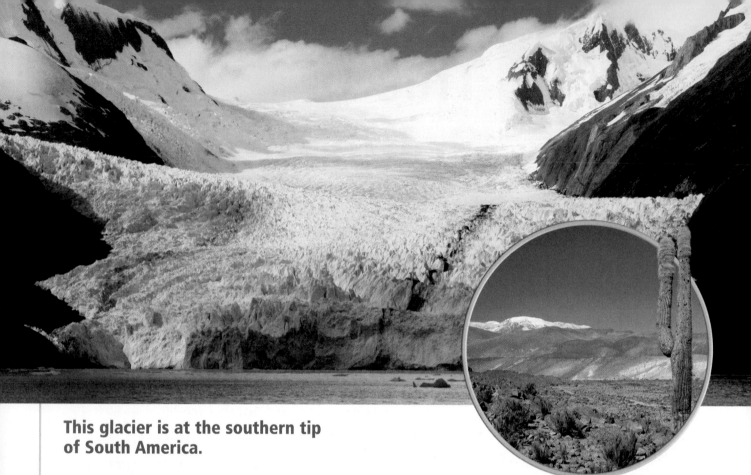

**This glacier is at the southern tip of South America.**

**Atacama Desert, northern Chile**

# South America's Geography

South America has many different landforms and bodies of water. The Andes Mountains stretch more than 5,000 miles along South America's west coast. They have both glaciers and volcanoes. A **glacier** is a huge mass of slow-moving ice.

The driest place on Earth, the Atacama Desert, is west of the Andes. To the east is one of the world's wettest places, the Amazon rain forest. South of the rain forest are grassy plains called the Pampas.

The Amazon rain forest is located in the Amazon River Basin. The basin works like a huge tub, with the Amazon River as a drain. The river is almost 4,000 miles long and has more than 1,000 tributaries. A **tributary** is a smaller river that flows into a larger one. The Amazon connects people who live thousands of miles apart.

main
(★)
idea

## South America's Landforms

Caribbean Sea

Panama Canal

ATLANTIC OCEAN

Orinoco River

Magdalena R.

Angel Falls

Casiquiare River

AMAZON

Amazon River

Galápagos Islands

Guayas River

Marañón R.

RAIN FOREST

Ucayali R.

São Francisco R.

ANDES

Lake Titicaca

BRAZILIAN HIGHLANDS

**KEY**

Mountains

Hills

Plateaus

Plains

▲ Highest point

⚡ Waterfall

Atacama Desert

Lake Poopó

Paraguay River

Paraná River

Mt. Aconcagua

PAMPAS

Patos Lagoon

ATLANTIC OCEAN

Easter Island

Lake Nahuel Huapí

Rio de la Plata

PACIFIC OCEAN

km 0   400   800
mi 0      400      800

Falkland Islands

Strait of Magellan

South Georgia Island

Scotia Sea

What islands are part of South America?

**South America** South America has highlands, lowlands, and plains.

Other big rivers are the Orinoco River and the Paraguay-Paraná River. To the south, the Strait of Magellan connects the Atlantic and Pacific oceans. A **strait** is a narrow waterway that connects two big bodies of water. North of South America, the Panama Canal also connects these oceans.

South America's mountains, deserts, and forests are difficult places to live. They are often a barrier to people. Most people in South America live near a river or a coast. It is easier to farm, trade, and move around there.

✓**READING CHECK** CAUSE AND EFFECT Why do most people in South America live near a river or an ocean?

# Climate, Plants, and Animals

Three main climate regions in South America are home main (★) idea to many plants and animals. The higher elevations in the Andes have cold weather with mixed sun and snow. **Elevation** means how high above sea level a place is. Llamas, vicuñas (veye KOO nuh), condors, and cougars live here. Vicuñas and other mammals graze the grassy meadows of the high Andes.

The center of the continent has mild winters, warm summers, and rain most of the year. Forests and grass grow here. Giant anteaters, foxes, skunks, deer, and rhea live here. The rhea is a flightless bird similar to an ostrich.

The Amazon rain forest has a tropical climate. It is hot and rainy all year long. So many plants and animals live here that not all of them have been discovered yet! Trees here sometimes grow 13 stories tall. There are vines, shrubs, and mushrooms. Vampire bats, macaw parrots, jaguars, and capybaras live here.

Weighing about 100 pounds, the capybara is the world's largest rodent.

## Natural Resources

South America has many natural resources. The continent's metals include gold, copper, and tin. Other underground resources are oil and coal, which provide energy.

Farming and ranching are widespread in many South American countries. Fishing also plays an important role in their economies. Forests are important sources of wood.

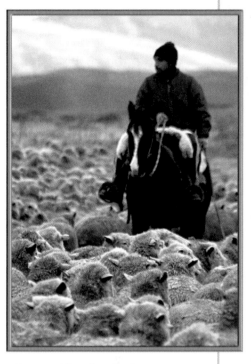

Argentina's plains are good for raising sheep.

✔**READING CHECK** MAIN IDEA AND DETAILS Give three details that support the main idea that South America has many different natural resources.

**SUMMARY**

South America has Earth's longest mountain range, driest desert, biggest rain forest, and river with the most water. South America has three main climates and valuable natural resources.

## Lesson Review

**1** **WHAT TO KNOW** What are some of South America's geographic features?

**2** **VOCABULARY** Use **glacier** and **elevation** in a sentence about the Andes Mountains.

**3** **CRITICAL THINKING: Synthesize** How do waterways connect and separate people and places in South America?

**4** **ART ACTIVITY** Sketch a South American animal in its habitat.

**5** 🖋 **CAUSE AND EFFECT** Complete the graphic organizer to show how South America's geographic features affect people.

## Skillbuilder

# Use Latitude and Longitude

▶ **VOCABULARY**

latitude

equator

hemisphere

longitude

prime meridian

You can tell the exact location of different places on Earth by using the latitude and longitude lines on a map or globe. These lines form a grid on maps and globes.

## Learn the Skill

**Step 1:** Lines that cross the globe from side to side are **latitude** lines. The **equator** is a line of latitude that circles the globe exactly halfway between the North and South poles. It divides Earth into two hemispheres. A **hemisphere** is one half of Earth's surface. Latitude lines north of the equator are in the northern hemisphere. They are labeled *N*. Lines to the south are in the southern hemisphere. They are labeled *S*.

**Step 2:** The lines that cross the globe from top to bottom are **longitude** lines. The **prime meridian** is a longitude line that passes through Greenwich, England. The prime meridian divides Earth into eastern and western hemispheres. Longitude lines to the east of the prime meridian are labeled *E*. Those to the west are labeled *W*.

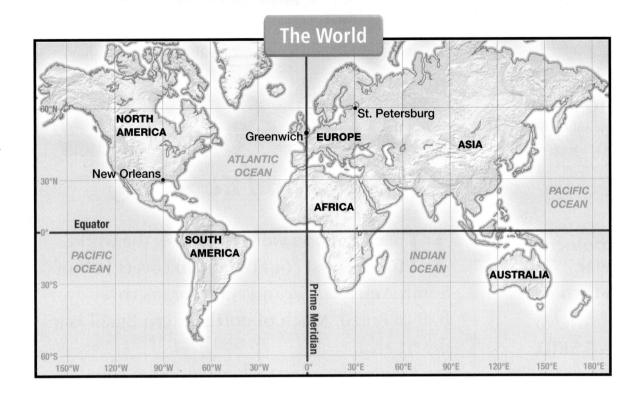

The World

60°N

NORTH AMERICA

St. Petersburg

Greenwich   EUROPE

ASIA

ATLANTIC OCEAN

30°N

New Orleans

PACIFIC OCEAN

AFRICA

Equator

0°

SOUTH AMERICA

PACIFIC OCEAN

INDIAN OCEAN

AUSTRALIA

30°S

Prime Meridian

60°S

150°W   120°W   90°W   60°W   30°W   0°   30°E   60°E   90°E   120°E   150°E   180°E

## Practice the Skill

Use the world map above to answer each question.

**1** Which city is located on the prime meridian?

**2** What are the latitude and longitude for New Orleans, Louisiana? for St. Petersburg, Russia?

**3** Is Australia in the northern or southern hemisphere?

## Apply the Skill

Pick three places on a classroom globe or map. Write down their latitude and longitude numbers. Then ask a classmate to use latitude and longitude to find each place, and state whether it is in the eastern or western hemisphere.

# Lesson 2

▶ **WHAT TO KNOW**
How do people in Brazil use natural resources?

▶ **VOCABULARY**
bay
hydroelectric power
high-tech

✪ **READING SKILL**
**Generalize** As you read, list facts and make a generalization about the different kinds of jobs Brazilians have.

# BRAZIL
## *Land and Economy*

Huge is a good word for Brazil, the world's fifth-largest country. Brazil covers half of South America. Gigantic rain forests cover over half of Brazil. Much of northeastern Brazil is a desert area.

Geography affects where and how people live. Only a few cities are located in Brazil's rain forests and desert. Most Brazilians live in southern and southeastern Brazil. This region has low mountains, excellent farmlands, and protected bays. A **bay** is part of an ocean or of a lake that extends into the land.

*main idea* (★)

**Rio de Janeiro and other cities surround Guanabara Bay.**

## Climate and Resources

Like other places on the equator, Brazil has a tropical climate. That means it is hot and rainy.

Brazil's rain falls on forests that supply timber, rubber, and nuts. It falls on farms where sugar cane, coffee, bananas, or corn grow. It collects in thousands of rivers. Some large rivers are a source of hydroelectric power. **Hydroelectric power** is electricity created by moving water.

Brazil has a long coastline along the Atlantic Ocean, with many ports and beaches. Its interior, the region away from the coast, is rich in minerals.

**✔ READING CHECK** GENERALIZE Give two facts to support the generalization that water is an important resource in Brazil.

**Brazil's Landforms**

GUIANA HIGHLANDS
Pico de Neblina
Branco River
Negro River
Amazon River
ATLANTIC OCEAN
AMAZON
Madeira River
BASIN
BRAZIL
São Francisco River
BRAZILIAN
HIGHLANDS
Paraná River
Iguaçu Falls
ATLANTIC OCEAN

N W E S

**KEY**
- Mountains
- Hills
- Plateaus
- Plains
- ▲ Highest point
- ⟋ Waterfall
- —— National border

km 0   250   500
mi 0   250   500

? What is the highest point in Brazil?

## Brazil's Economy

Service jobs are the most common jobs in Brazil. Service workers include teachers, doctors, nurses, government workers, cooks, waiters, and others who serve people's needs. Other Brazilians work in manufacturing. They work in factories, making everything from food products, fabrics, and cement to high-tech computers and airplanes. **High-tech** stands for "high technology." It means using advanced scientific knowledge to get work done.

Other Brazilians work on farms and ranches. They grow crops such as oranges, coffee, sugar cane, and cacao for chocolate. They also raise livestock such as cattle, sheep, and goats. In Brazil, as in the United States, people are free to work for whatever business they choose. However, the government of Brazil also gives extra help to some businesses, such as the high-tech and steel industries. The government helps these businesses because it believes they can help the Brazilian economy grow.

✔**READING CHECK** CAUSE AND EFFECT What effect should the Brazilian government's helping high-tech and steel industries have?

**?** Which product or industry shown on the map is located in the Amazon Basin?

VENEZUELA

COLOMBIA

PERU

*Forest Products*
Brazilians take many products from the Amazon rain forests. Here a worker collects sap from a rubber tree near Manicoré. The white sap is used to manufacture rubber.

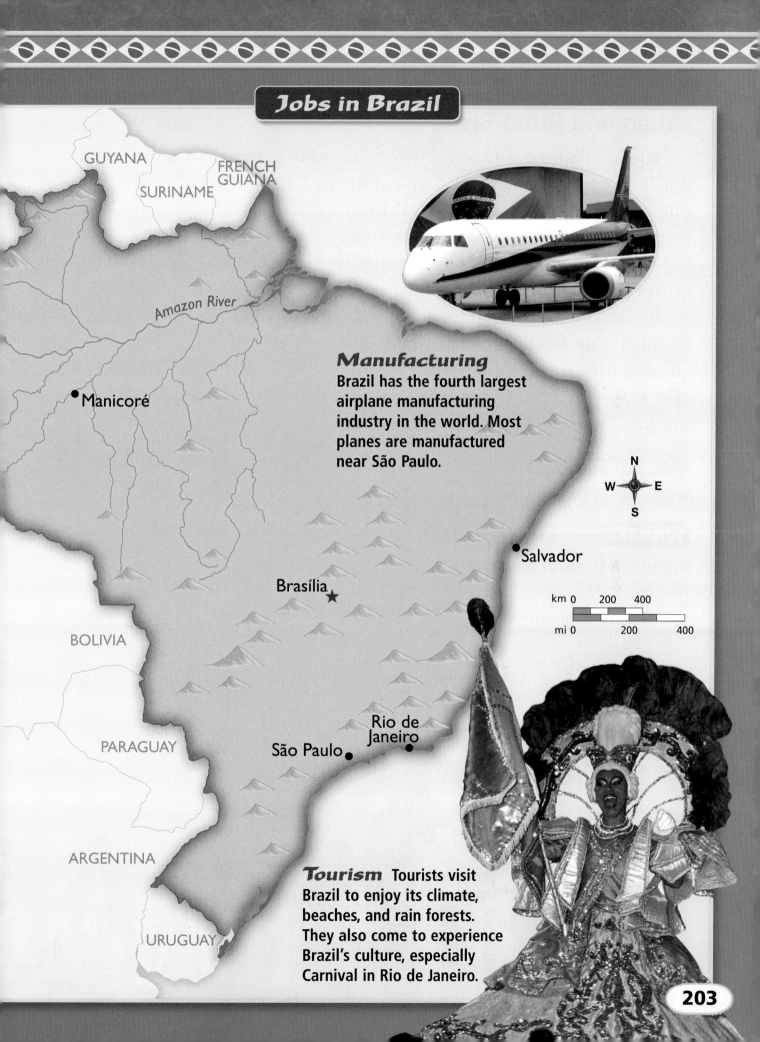

GUYANA

FRENCH GUIANA

SURINAME

Amazon River

•Manicoré

## Manufacturing
Brazil has the fourth largest airplane manufacturing industry in the world. Most planes are manufactured near São Paulo.

N
W E
S

•Salvador

Brasília ★

km 0   200   400
mi 0   200   400

BOLIVIA

PARAGUAY

Rio de Janeiro
•

São Paulo •

ARGENTINA

URUGUAY

## Tourism
Tourists visit Brazil to enjoy its climate, beaches, and rain forests. They also come to experience Brazil's culture, especially Carnival in Rio de Janeiro.

203

## Urban and Rural Brazil

<u>Life in urban areas is very different from life in rural Brazil.</u> In cities such as São Paulo and Rio de Janeiro, life is often fast-paced and busy. Modern skyscrapers are crowded together. Many people live in tall apartment buildings with little light and no gardens. Stores, restaurants, factories, and offices provide many jobs.

*main idea*

In rural areas, life is more slow-paced. Towns are less crowded. Families live in houses rather than apartments. Some houses are built from stone or from adobe, a type of clay. Most have a yard. Most people work on farms and ranches. Others fish or harvest nuts or rubber.

**✓ READING CHECK** COMPARE AND CONTRAST What are two ways that urban Brazil is different from rural Brazil?

**SUMMARY**

Brazil is a tropical country. It has many valuable resources. Many Brazilians work in service jobs, manufacturing, agriculture, forestry, or fishing.

**Brazil's cities range from small rural towns to crowded São Paulo.**

# CASE STUDY REVIEW

## ❶ What to Know

How do people in Brazil use natural resources?

## ❷ Reading Skill  Generalize

Complete the graphic organizer to generalize about the kinds of jobs Brazilians have.

## ❸ Case Study Detective

Can you guess what delicious treat you get when the bottom part of this fruit is roasted and salted? In Portuguese it's called *caju* (kah ZHOO). Hint: One of the scrambled words below is the answer.

## ❹ Word Play

Unscramble the letters to find products from Brazil.

fcfeoe        nroages        wahsce

rbrueb        snalirepa        accoa

Write a sentence using three of the words.

# Hi-Tech Brazil

**Have you ever talked to someone far away?** Millions of Brazilians use cell phones and the Internet to communicate. People in Brazil and other parts of the world depend on satellites. A satellite is a machine that travels in space, getting and sending information, such as television or telephone signals.

In the Amazon River basin, Brazil has built a launching center for satellites called Alcântara (ow KAHN tuh ruh). It is located close to the equator, where the ground moves faster as Earth spins. This helps move the rockets and satellites into space more easily. That makes Brazil an ideal location for launching satellites.

## Communication

Communication satellites send messages from one part of the world to another. They help students use the Internet.

## Navigation

Satellites help scientists track and study jaguars. Some jaguars wear radio collars that allow scientists to follow their daily activities.

## Weather

Weather satellites send pictures of Earth to weather forecasters. These pictures help predict the weather.

## Activities

1. **TALK ABOUT IT** What things do you do that depend on information from satellites?

2. **WRITE ABOUT IT** If you could design a satellite to help you with tasks on Earth, what would your satellite do? Write a paragraph telling about it.

# BRAZIL
## History and Government

### ▶ WHAT TO KNOW
What are some key events in Brazil's history?

### ▶ VOCABULARY
**hunter-gatherer**
**claim**
**monarchy**
**modernize**

### ◎ READING SKILL
**Sequence** As you read, list events in Brazil's history in the order that they happened.

| | |
|---|---|
| 1 | |
| 2 | |
| 3 | |
| 4 | |

The Yanomami are a South American Indian group that lives near the Orinoco River in Brazil. They are hunter-gatherers. A **hunter-gatherer** is a person who hunts animals and gathers plants for food. The Yanomami hunt deer and gather fruits, nuts, and honey. They also grow crops such as bananas and corn. The Yanomami are one of about 200 Indian groups living in Brazil today.

Over 500 years ago, about 1,000 Indian groups lived in the area now called Brazil. Those groups were hunter-gatherers. Their lives changed greatly when people from Europe arrived.

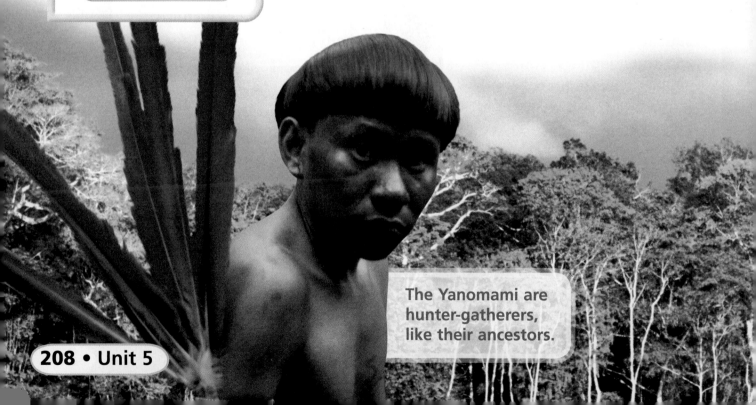

The Yanomami are hunter-gatherers, like their ancestors.

## Portugal Claims Brazil

In 1500, Pedro Álvares Cabral and his crew sailed from Portugal to Brazil. They were the first Europeans to reach the area, so they claimed it for Portugal. To **claim** something is to say you own it. The Portuguese did not settle in Brazil at first. Instead, they traded metal goods, such as tools and cooking pots, to the Indians for brazilwood. Brazilwood was a source of dye used to color cloth red.

In the 1530s, the King of Portugal gave some Portuguese colonists large areas of land in Brazil to plant sugar cane. Making and selling sugar made the colonists rich, but hurt other people. Colonists forced American Indians and later Africans to work as slaves on their farms.

At first, the colonists lived only along the northeastern coast. Then, in the 1600s, explorers discovered gold farther west. Suddenly, people hurried inland to mine for gold. Few found it, and many became ranchers or farmers instead.

**✔ READING CHECK** SEQUENCE Who were the first people to live in Brazil? Who came later?

Pedro Álvares Cabral and his crew were the first Europeans in Brazil.

## Brazil Becomes Independent

Brazil was a Portuguese colony for about 300 years. In the 1820s, many Brazilians wanted Brazil to become an independent country. At that time, the Portuguese king's son, Pedro, was in charge of Brazil. Pedro had grown up in Brazil and loved the Brazilian people. He agreed to declare Brazil independent from Portugal.

Pedro I ruled Brazil as a monarchy. A **monarchy** is a country ruled by a king or queen. In 1831, Pedro I left his son, Pedro II, in charge of Brazil. Pedro II modernized Brazil by building railroads, selling rubber to other countries, and helping cities grow. To **modernize** means to make something up-to-date.

Another important change occurred during Pedro II's rule. In 1888, the Golden Law was signed. This law ended slavery in Brazil. The Golden Law made landowners unhappy, since they now had to pay their workers.

### Important Dates in Brazil's History

1750          1800          1850

**1822**
Brazil becomes independent under Pedro I.

**1889**
Brazil becomes a republic.

## A More Modern Government

The landowners joined with others who wanted to end the monarchy. In 1889, they forced Pedro II to give up power. Brazil became a republic led by an elected president. Only a small number of people had the right to vote, however.

Over the next 100 years, Brazil continued to grow. In 1960, the president decided to move the capital from Rio de Janeiro on the coast to a brand new city in the center of the country. He had a new capital built and named it Brasília. Brasília's modern architecture and new buildings made Brazilians proud of their nation.

Though the country grew, people still had little say in their government. In 1988, leaders wrote a new constitution that made Brazil more democratic.

**✓ READING CHECK** CAUSE AND EFFECT What was the effect of Brazil's constitution of 1988?

**Skill** **Reading Timelines** In what year did Brazil become a republic?

1900      1950      2000

**1960**
Brasília becomes Brazil's capital city.

**1989**
Under a new constitution, Brazilians elect President Fernando Collor de Mello.

City of Brasília

## Brazil's Government Today

Today, Brazil is a federal republic. That means that Brazil has states that have their own governments. Brazil has 26 states, plus the Federal District of Brasília.

Brazil's government is similar to the United States' government. One branch, the congress, makes laws. Another branch, headed by the president, makes sure the laws are followed. The third branch, the courts, settles disagreements about the laws. One of the government's biggest challenges is to improve the lives of Brazil's many poor people.

**main idea** ( ★ )

✓**READING CHECK** COMPARE AND CONTRAST

How is Brazil's government similar to the United States' government?

**SUMMARY**

South American Indians were Brazil's first people. Through its history, Brazil has been a colony, a monarchy, and a republic.

Brazil's President Luiz Inácio Lula da Silva

| Voting in Brazil and the United States | | |
|---|---|---|
| **Subject** | **Brazil** | **United States** |
| How old do you have to be to vote? | 16 years old | 18 years old |
| Is voting required by law? | Yes | No, but it is a right and a duty |
| Are all voting machines computerized? | Yes, the first country in the world to do so | Depends on the state and local governments |

# ❶ What to Know

What are some key events in Brazil's history?

# ❷ Reading Skill Sequence

Complete the graphic organizer to sequence events in Brazil's history.

| 1 | |
|---|---|
| 2 | |
| 3 | |
| 4 | |

# ❸ Case Study Detective

Look at these pictures of Brasília. What are three words you would use to descibe this city?

# ❹ Word Play

Use the clues to figure out a mystery phrase about Brazil's history.

• Many landowners were angered by it.

• It passed in 1888.

• It ended slavery in Brazil.

\_ \_ E    G \_ \_ \_ E \_    \_ A \_

# Visiting the Amazon Rain Forest

**Have you ever read about a place you've never visited?** In the 1800s, few people from the United States had seen or even knew about Brazil's Amazon rain forest. But they could learn about it by reading.

In 1846, New Yorker William H. Edwards traveled to Brazil to study nature there. When he returned home, he wrote a book about his trip.

Edwards described the animals, trees, plants, and flowers he saw in the rain forest. He called the Amazon the "garden of the world." Today, Edwards's words give a picture of life in the Amazon at that time.

William H. Edwards (1822–1909) was born in Hunter, New York. His book on the Amazon inspired others to explore the river and rain forest.

Trees of incredible [thickness] tower aloft [high up in the air]. . . . The trunks are of every variety of form. . . . Amid these giants very few low trees or little underbrush interfere with one's movements. . . . But about the trees cling huge snake-like vines, winding round and round the trunks, and through the branches sending their long arms, [tying] tree to tree. . . . In this way the whole forest is linked together, and a cut tree rarely falls without involving the destruction of many others.

From *A Voyage Up the River Amazon*, by William H. Edwards, 1847

## Activities

1. **TALK ABOUT IT** What descriptive words did Edwards use to describe the trees in the Amazon rain forest?

2. **WRITE ABOUT IT** Write a short story about someone's first visit to your school. How might the visitor describe your classroom?

 Visit Education Place for more primary sources.
www.eduplace.com/nycssp/

# Point of View

▶ **VOCABULARY**

point of view

Brazil has a democratic form of government. In a democracy, people are free to express their points of view. A point of view is the way a person thinks about an issue. Sharing your point of view is an important part of living in a democracy.

## Learn the Skill

Follow the steps below to share your point of view.

**Step 1:** Read or listen carefully to other people's points of view about a subject. If possible, ask questions about anything you do not understand.

**Step 2:** Think about what other people have said. Is it similar to what you think? In what ways is it different?

**Step 3:** Using the information you gathered, write or tell about your point of view.

Town meeting tonight at 7 pm

## Practice the Skill

Suppose there is an empty lot in your community. A group of people agree that the space should be used for the good of the whole community. They have different points of view about how to use the space, though. Read the points of view below, and then answer the questions.

"This lot would be a good place for sports. We could have a volleyball or basketball court."

"It would be a great place for a stage. We could build rows of benches and have plays and concerts."

"We could plant flowers and vegetables and watch them grow most of the year. We could also build bird feeders."

**1** Summarize each opinion in your own words.

**2** What is one question that you might ask about each opinion?

**3** Which idea do you agree with the most? Explain why.

## Apply the Skill

Write a paragraph to share your own point of view about how to use the lot. Make sure to give reasons why you have this point of view.

▶ **WHAT TO KNOW**
What are some cultural traditions in Brazil?

▶ **VOCABULARY**
**immigration**
**extended family**
**popular music**
**leisure time**

**READING SKILL**
**Main Idea and Details** As you read, note a main idea and three details about Brazil's culture.

# BRAZIL
## People and Culture

Brazil has more people than all the rest of South America together. Brazil's people reflect their country's history. South American Indians were the first Brazilians. Then, Portuguese settlers came to Brazil. Later, millions of Africans were forced to come to Brazil as slaves. Today, most Brazilians have Indian, Portuguese, and African ancestors.

*main idea*

In the 1900s, immigration from Germany, Italy, Spain, Syria, Lebanon, and Japan brought new people to Brazil. **Immigration** means moving to a new country. Brazil's culture includes traditions from all these people.

**Two Brazilian families**

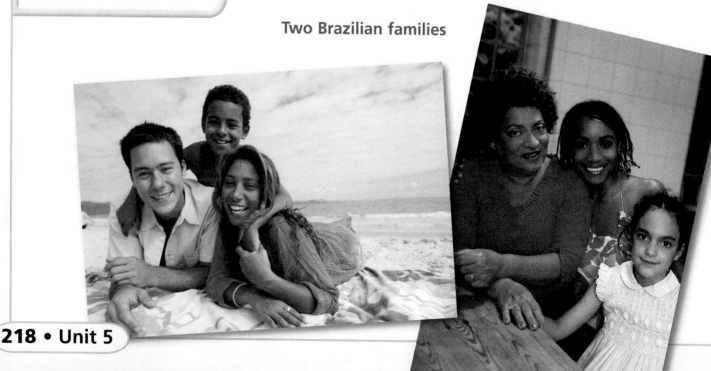

## Family and Faith in Brazil

In Brazil, family comes first. When Brazilians speak of family, they often mean their extended family. An **extended family** includes grandparents, aunts, uncles, cousins, and others. Many Brazilian families have a lot of children. Urban families may be smaller than rural families. Families stay close by eating meals together. Seafood, rice, black beans, and fresh fruit are popular foods in Brazil.

For many Brazilian families, attending church is an important part of spending time together. Brazil has more Roman Catholics than any other country in the world. Some Brazilians also practice religions that started in Brazil, such as Candomblé (kahn dom BLAY). Candomblé blends beliefs from African religions with Catholic beliefs. Protestants, Jews, and Buddhists also live in Brazil.

This Catholic church in Northeast Brazil was begun in 1704. It took nearly 100 years to finish.

✓ **READING CHECK** MAIN IDEA AND DETAILS Give three details that show how family is important to Brazilians.

These girls are taking part in a Candomblé ceremony.

## Brazil's Culture

Brazilian culture grew out of Portuguese, Indian, and African traditions. During the 1700s and 1800s, Brazil's culture was a lot like Portugal's. For example, Antônio Francisco Lisboa was a great Brazilian architect and sculptor. His buildings and statues would not have looked out of place in Portugal.

main idea ⭐

By the 1900s, Brazilians were creating a culture that was very much their own. Writers like Mário de Andrade (ahn DRAH jee) wrote about subjects that were important to ordinary Brazilians. Here is one of his poems:

> Who's playing today? The Paulistano Team.
> Off to the America Garden of the roses and kick-offs!
> Friedenreich made a goal! Corner! What a referee!

In the 1950s, Brazil gave the world *bossa nova* music. Bossa nova combines American jazz with Brazilian samba music. The samba is a Brazilian dance with African roots. Bossa nova is one of many forms of Brazilian popular music. **Popular music** means tunes and songs that many people enjoy listening to. "The Girl from Ipanema" (ee pah NAY muh) is a world-famous bossa nova song.

✔**READING CHECK** DRAW CONCLUSIONS What was Mário de Andrade's poem about?

**Popular Music** Astrud Gilberto (1940– ) is best known for singing bossa nova songs. Her recording of "The Girl from Ipanema" made her famous in the United States.

**Painting** Tarsila do Amaral (1886–1973) was part of a group of Brazilian artists who wanted to separate Brazilian culture from European culture. She painted things that were found only in Brazil. She painted bright colors that seemed Brazilian to her.

Carnival in Madureira

**Capoeira** Enslaved Africans in Brazil invented this form of martial arts that is also a game and a dance. Capoeira (kah poo AY ruh) uses back bends, hand stands, and head spins, all set to its own style of music.

## School and Fun

Students in Brazil enjoy school and leisure time. **Leisure time** means free time. In school, Brazilian students learn to read and write Portuguese. They study history, geography, math, and science. All children between the ages of seven and fourteen have to go to school. Only about one in five students goes on to high school after turning fourteen.

After school, many Brazilian young people enjoy playing soccer. In Brazil, soccer is called *futebol* (foo chee BOW). Brazilians also enjoy watching professional soccer. Brazil's national team has won the World Cup five times.

On weekends, many Brazilians go to the beach to swim, fish, and play in the sand. Brazil's tropical beaches are busy all year long.

**main idea**

✓ **READING CHECK** COMPARE AND CONTRAST How are students in Brazil like students you know?

**SUMMARY**

Brazil's people and culture are a mixture of American Indian, African, and Portuguese roots.

### School Calendar in Brazil

| Date | Event |
|------|-------|
| February 11th | First Day of School |
| July 7th to July 25th | Winter Break |
| September 7th | Independence Day |
| December 5th | Last Day of School |

In Brazil, it is summer from January to March. The school year begins in February.

### ❶ What to Know

What are some cultural traditions in Brazil?

### ❷ Reading Skill  Main Idea and Details

Complete the graphic organizer to
show the main idea and details.

Brazil has a mix of cultures.

### ❸ Case Study Detective

What is happening in this photo?

### ❹ Word Play

The word *immigrate* means "to move <u>to</u> a new country." The
word *emigrate* means "to move <u>from</u> a country." Both words
contain *migrate*. Can you guess what *migrate* means?
Use the letters of *migrate* to spell other words. Here are three:

gram    term    timer

How many more can you spell?

# Brazil

**Celebremos!** Brazilians celebrate many holidays with family parties, parades, dances, and music. Each region in Brazil has special holidays, but Carnival is celebrated everywhere.

**Brazil's Flag**

Brazil's motto *Ordem e Progresso* means *Order and Progress.*

This pattern of stars shows the groups of stars you can see in the night sky over Brazil.

**Brazil's Flag and Seal** This flag and seal use the same colors and some of the same symbols to represent Brazil. The 27 stars stand for Brazil's 26 states and the one Federal District.

**Brazil's Seal**

## Independence Day

Brazil declared its independence from Portugal on September 7, 1822. Brazilians celebrate the anniversary of this day with parades. Many people wear the green and yellow colors of the Brazilian flag and eat the Brazilian national dish, black beans and rice, on this holiday.

## June Festivals

Communities honor several Catholic saints and celebrate rural life during the June Festivals. People dress up in old-fashioned clothes, paint freckles on their faces, and wear straw hats. They dance square dances and eat food made from corn. At night there are bonfires.

## Carnival

Forty days before Easter, Brazil celebrates Carnival. Carnival is a four-day-long party. Social clubs called "samba schools" parade through Brazil's cities, competing for the best costumes, floats, dances, and music. Samba (SAHM buh) is the style of dance music played for Carnival.

**?** How do Brazilians celebrate Carnival?

# Marina Silva

**How do you know when it is going to rain?** Brazilian Senator Marina Silva learned to predict the weather by watching ants. If the ants crawled up the anthill to higher ground, a storm was probably on its way.

While growing up in the Amazon rain forest, Silva and her family depended on their knowledge of nature for survival. She helped her father fish and collect sap from rubber trees. But the forest was changing and resources were getting harder to find. People cut down many trees for lumber or to make fields where cows could graze.

For five years, Silva was Brazil's Minister of Environment. She worked with other government officials to make laws. She looked for ways that Brazilians could use the Amazon's resources while preserving the rain forest for the animals and people who live there.

Senator Silva helps people find ways to use the rain-forest resources responsibly. She wants people to be able to enjoy the Amazon in the future.

"I want to see the best of modern times, but also the best of tradition, the anthill from below and from above. It is the marriage between tradition and modernity, between city and forest, sky and earth that will make Brazil into the nation we seek."

— Marina Silva

The Amazon rain forest contains over one million different kinds of insects, birds, animals, and plants.

## Activities

1. **TALK ABOUT IT** Why does Silva believe it is important to protect the Amazon rain forest?

2. **WRITE ABOUT IT** Write a letter to Marina Silva. In your letter, suggest ways that you can help protect the environment where you live.

# Fun with Social Studies

## Where Are You?

Name where you are in South America.

These mountains stretch for more than 5,000 miles along South America's west coast. They have glaciers and active volcanoes. Where are you?

This area is hot and rainy all year long. Some of the trees are 200 feet tall! There are many kinds of animals here, including bats, parrots, and jaguars. Where are you?

This river has more water than any other river on Earth! It is almost 4,000 miles long and has more than 1,000 tributaries. Where are you?

# Missing Letters

**VOCABULARY**

Use the missing letters to answer the riddle.

## Word

gl?cier

elevatio?

hun?er-gatherer

lei?ure time

## Clue

a huge mass of slow-moving ice

how high a place is above sea level

a person who hunts animals and gathers plants for food

free time

**What do uncles find at picnics?**

? ? ? ?

Go Digital

# Education Place®
## www.eduplace.com

**World Communities Now and Long Ago**

eGlossary

eWord Game

Biographies

Primary Sources

Write Site

Interactive Maps

GeoGlossary

GeoNet

Online Atlas

## Visit Eduplace!

Log on to Eduplace to explore Social Studies online. Solve puzzles to watch the skateboarding tricks in eWord Game. Join Chester in GeoNet to see if you can earn enough points to become a GeoChampion, or just play Wacky Web Tales to see how silly your stories can get. Play now at **www.eduplace.com/nycssp/**

# Reading Social Studies

**Causes** are events that bring about changes. When we ask why something happened, the answer is a **cause**. **Effects** are things that happen because of some reason.

## Cause and Effect

1. Complete the graphic organizer to show that you understand important causes and effects in the history of Brazil.

| | → | Millions of enslaved Africans were brought to Brazil. |

| Gold was discovered in the west. | → | |

| Brazilian leaders wanted to modernize the country. | → | |

# Write About the Big Idea

2. **Write a Dialogue** Culture, history, geography, people, and government all affect communities in South America. Write a dialogue between two people who are talking about Brazil's history. Each person should choose one historical event and explain how it affected Brazilians' lives.

## Vocabulary and Main Ideas

**Write a sentence to answer each question.**

3. What geographical feature divides South America and has **glaciers**?

4. Why is **hydroelectric power** important in Brazil?

5. How do **hunter-gatherers** get their food?

6. What effect did **immigration** have on Brazil?

## Critical Thinking

**Write a short answer for each question.**

7. **Fact and Opinion** Give your own opinion about life in Brazil. Then, give two facts that support your opinion.

8. **Compare and Contrast** How is the history of Brazil similar to the history of the United States? How is it different?

## Apply Skills

**Use Latitude and Longitude**
Use the map of South America to answer each question.

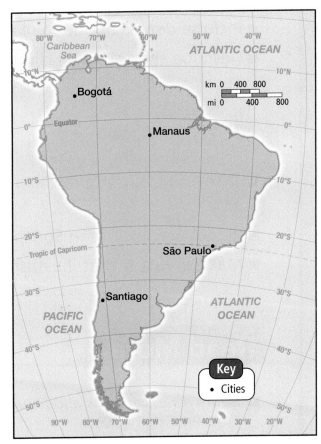

9. In what hemisphere is most of South America located?

10. Which city is at about 23° S latitude, on the Tropic of Capricorn?

   A. Bogotá

   B. Manaus

   C. São Paulo

   D. Santiago

# Unit 5 Activities

 ## Unit Writing Activity

**Write a Letter** Write a letter to someone describing Brazil's geographic features.

■ Include details about the kinds of land and water in Brazil.

■ Describe the country's climate and natural resources.

 ## Unit Project

**Culture Fair** Create fair exhibits about cultures in South America.

■ Research a culture in South America.

■ Make a poster that illustrates the customs of the culture.

## Read More

■ *South America: Facts and Figures,* by Roger E. Hernández. Mason Crest Publishers, 2003.

■ *Brazil: An Awakening Giant,* by Mark L. Carpenter. Dillon Press, 1997.

■ *A Visit to Colombia,* by Mary Virginia Fox. Heinemann, 2000.

 visit www.eduplace.com/nycssp/

# Resources

The Five Themes of Geography . . . . . . . . . . . R2

Atlas . . . . . . . . . . . . . . . . . . . . . . . . . . . . . . R4

Glossary . . . . . . . . . . . . . . . . . . . . . . . . . . . R24

Index . . . . . . . . . . . . . . . . . . . . . . . . . . . . . . R29

Acknowledgments . . . . . . . . . . . . . . . . . . . . R36

# The Five Themes of Geography

Learning about places is an important part of history and geography. **Geography** is the study of Earth's surface and the ways people use it.

When geographers study Earth, they often think about five main themes, or topics. Keep these themes in mind as you read. They will help you think like a geographer.

GEOGRAPHY

## Location

Everything on Earth has its own **location**—the place where it can be found.

## Place

Every place has physical and human characteristics, or features, that make it different from all other places. **Physical features** are formed by nature. **Human features** are created by people.

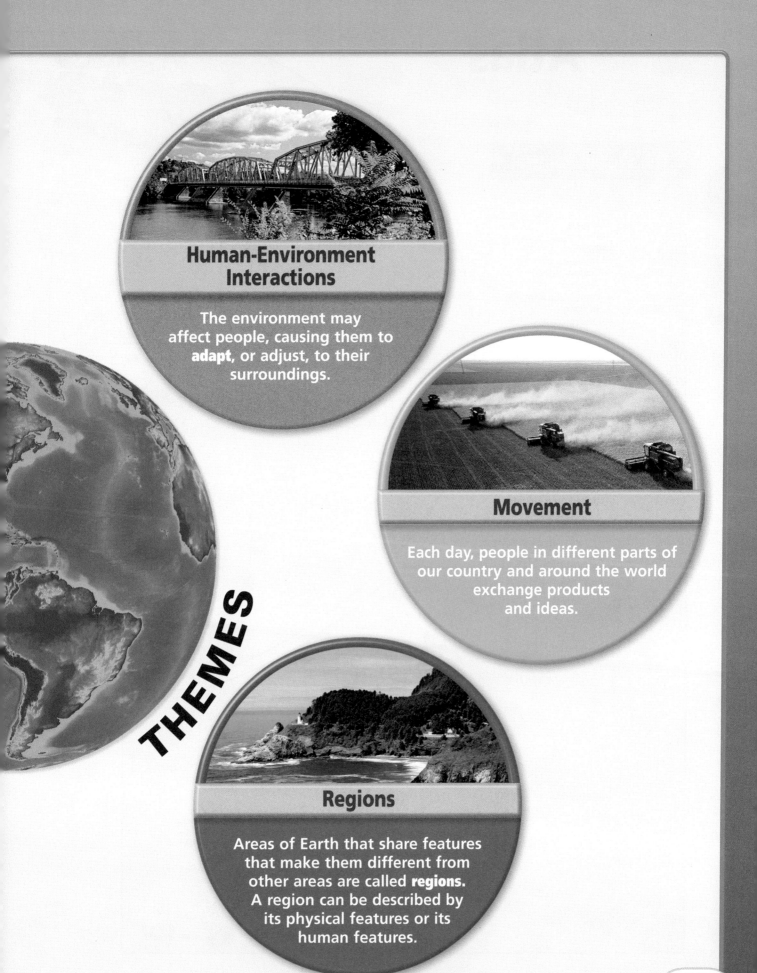

**Human-Environment Interactions**

The environment may affect people, causing them to **adapt**, or adjust, to their surroundings.

**Movement**

Each day, people in different parts of our country and around the world exchange products and ideas.

**THEMES**

**Regions**

Areas of Earth that share features that make them different from other areas are called **regions**. A region can be described by its physical features or its human features.

# Atlas

## The World: Political

| | |
|---|---|
| ALB. | —Albania |
| AZER. | —Azerbaijan |
| BOS. & HERZ. | —Bosnia & Herzegovina |
| CEN. AFR. REP. | —Central African Republic |
| DEM. REP. OF CONGO | —Democratic Republic of Congo |
| FR. | —France |
| IT. | —Italy |
| KOS. | —Kosovo |
| LIECH. | —Liechtenstein |
| LUX. | —Luxembourg |
| MONT. | —Montenegro |
| NETH. | —Netherlands |
| N.Z. | —New Zealand |
| N. KOREA | —North Korea |
| REP. OF CONGO | —Republic of Congo |
| SERB. | —Serbia |
| SLOV. | —Slovenia |
| S. KOREA | —South Korea |
| SWITZ. | —Switzerland |
| U.A.E. | —United Arab Emirates |
| U.K. | —United Kingdom |
| U.S. | —United States |

ARCTIC OCEAN

ICELAND

Area of index

EUROPE

RUSSIA

ASIA

KAZAKHSTAN

UZBEKISTAN
KYRGYZSTAN

GEORGIA
ARMENIA
TURKEY
AZER.
TURKMENISTAN
TAJIKISTAN

MONGOLIA

N. KOREA
S. KOREA

JAPAN

PACIFIC
OCEAN

TUNISIA
CYPRUS
SYRIA
IRAQ
AFGHANISTAN
CHINA

MOROCCO
LEBANON
ISRAEL
JORDAN
IRAN
KUWAIT
PAKISTAN
BHUTAN
NEPAL
TAIWAN

ALGERIA
LIBYA
EGYPT
BAHRAIN
QATAR
U. A. E.
SAUDI
ARABIA
OMAN
BANGLADESH

WESTERN
SAHARA
(Morocco)
AFRICA
INDIA
MYANMAR

Northern
Mariana
Islands
(U.S.)

MARSHALL
ISLANDS

CAPE
VERDE
MAURITANIA
NIGER
CHAD
ERITREA
YEMEN
LAOS
THAILAND
VIETNAM
Guam (U.S.)

FEDERATED STATES
OF MICRONESIA

MALI
SUDAN
DJIBOUTI
CAMBODIA
PHILIPPINES
PALAU
KIRIBATI

SENEGAL
GAMBIA
GUINEA BISSAU
GUINEA
SIERRA
LEONE
LIBERIA
BURKINA
FASO
GHANA
TOGO
BENIN
NIGERIA
CEN.AFR.
REP.
ETHIOPIA
SOMALIA
SRI LANKA
MALDIVES
BRUNEI
MALAYSIA
SINGAPORE
NAURU

EQU.
GUINEA
CAMEROON
UGANDA
KENYA
PAPUA
NEW
GUINEA
SOLOMON
ISLANDS
TUVALU

SAO TOME
AND PRINCIPE
GABON
DEM.
REP. OF
CONGO
RWANDA
BURUNDI
TANZANIA
INDONESIA
EAST
TIMOR

VANUATU

ANGOLA
MALAWI
COMOROS
NEW
Caledonia
(Fr.)
FIJI

ZAMBIA
MOZAMBIQUE
INDIAN
OCEAN

NAMIBIA
ZIMBABWE
BOTSWANA
MADAGASCAR
MAURITIUS
Reunion
(Fr.)

AUSTRALIA

SOUTH AFRICA
SWAZILAND
LESOTHO

km 0    1000    2000
mi 0    1000    2000

NEW
ZEALAND

ATLANTIC
OCEAN

SOUTHERN OCEAN

ANTARCTICA

FINLAND
SWEDEN
NORWAY
RUSSIA

ESTONIA
LATVIA
LITHUANIA
RUSSIA
BELARUS

km 0  150  300
mi 0   150  300

NORTH
SEA
DENMARK

UNITED
KINGDOM
NETH.
GERMANY
POLAND

IRELAND
BELGIUM
LUX.
CZECH
REPUBLIC
SLOVAKIA
UKRAINE

LIECH.
AUSTRIA
HUNGARY
MOLDOVA

ATLANTIC
OCEAN
FRANCE
SWITZ.
SAN
MARINO
SLOV.
CROATIA
BOS. &
HERZ.
SERB.
ROMANIA

MONACO
MONT.
KOS.
BULGARIA

ANDORRA
ITALY
MACEDONIA
ALB.

PORTUGAL
Corsica
(Fr.)
Sardinia
(It.)
GREECE
TURKEY

Balearic
Islands
(Sp.)

SPAIN

Sicily (It.)

GIBRALTAR
(U.K.)
MEDITERRANEAN SEA

MOROCCO
ALGERIA
TUNISIA

Atlas

R5

Atlas

ARCTIC OCEAN

20°E 40°E 60°E 80°E 100°E 120°E 140°E 160°E 80°N

Barents
Sea

Ural Mountains

Yenisey River

Ob River

60°N

EUROPE

Northern European Plain

Volga River

ASIA

Sea of
Okhotsk

Lake
Baikal

Heilong River

North
Sea

Danube

Alps

Mt. Elbrus
18,510 ft.

Aral
Sea

Sea
of
Japan

40°N

Black Sea

Caucasus
Mountains

Caspian Sea

Mtns.

Mediterranean Sea

Himalaya Mountains
Mt. Everest
29,035 ft.

Huang He

PACIFIC
OCEAN

SAHARA

Red Sea

Ganges River

East
China
Sea

Chang Jiang

20°N

SAHEL

Nile River

Arabian
Sea

Bay of
Bengal

South
China
Sea

Philippine Islands

Micronesia

AFRICA

Niger River

Congo River

Lake
Victoria

Mt. Kilimanjaro
19,340 ft.

Sumatra

Borneo

Equator 0°

New Guinea

Melanesia

Java

INDIAN
OCEAN

Madagascar

Great
Sandy
Desert

Coral
Sea

20°S

Kalahari
Desert

AUSTRALIA

Darling River

Tasman
Sea

Cape of
Good Hope

Mt. Kosciusko
7,310 ft.

North Island

South Island

Prime Meridian

SOUTHERN
OCEAN

60°S

Antarctic Circle

ANTARCTICA

# United States: Political

## ALASKA inset

ARCTIC OCEAN

RUSSIA

ALASKA

CANADA

Yukon River

Fairbanks

Anchorage

Juneau

Aleutian Islands

PACIFIC OCEAN

km 0 250 500
mi 0 250 500

## Main map

Seattle

★ Olympia

WASHINGTON

Portland

★ Salem

OREGON

Columbia R.

Helena ★

MONTANA

Billings

IDAHO

★ Boise

Pocatello

Snake River

WYOMING

Casper

Cheyenne ★

Sacramento ★

Reno

★ Carson City

Salt Lake City ★

Provo

COLORADO

Denver ★

Colorado Springs

San Francisco

NEVADA

UTAH

Pueblo

PACIFIC OCEAN

CALIFORNIA

Las Vegas

Colorado River

Los Angeles

ARIZONA

Santa Fe ★

Albuquerque

San Diego

★ Phoenix

NEW MEXICO

Tucson

El Paso

Rio Grande

Gulf of California

MEXICO

### Compass

N W E S

### LEGEND

⊗ National capital

★ State capital

• Major city

— National boundary

— State boundary

## HAWAII inset

Kauai

HAWAII

Niihau

Oahu

Kailua

Molokai

Honolulu

Maui

Lanai

Kahoolawe

Hilo

Hawaii

PACIFIC OCEAN

km 0 50 100
mi 0 50 100

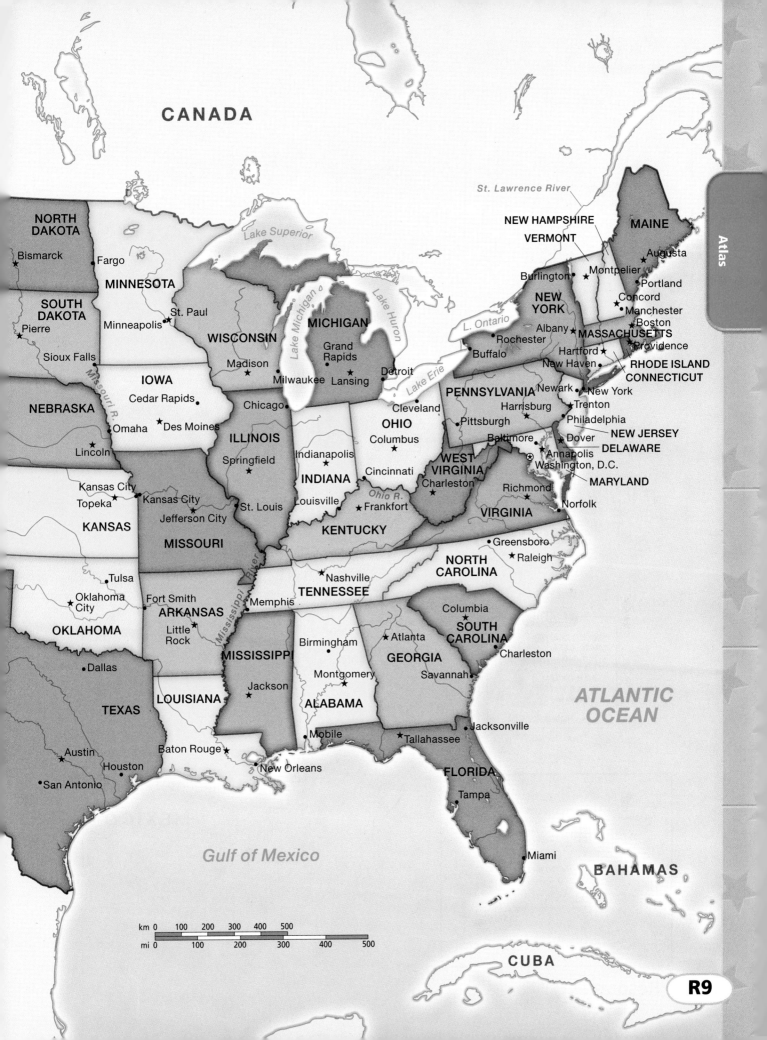

CANADA

**NORTH DAKOTA**
Bismarck
Fargo

**MINNESOTA**
St. Paul
Minneapolis

**SOUTH DAKOTA**
Pierre
Sioux Falls

Lake Superior

**WISCONSIN**
Madison
Milwaukee

**MICHIGAN**
Grand Rapids
Lansing
Detroit

Lake Michigan
Lake Huron
Lake Erie

St. Lawrence River

**NEW HAMPSHIRE**
**VERMONT**
Burlington
Montpelier
Concord
Manchester

**MAINE**
Augusta
Portland

**NEW YORK**
Albany
Rochester
Buffalo

L. Ontario

**MASSACHUSETTS**
Boston
Providence
Hartford
New Haven

**RHODE ISLAND**
**CONNECTICUT**

**IOWA**
Cedar Rapids
Des Moines

**NEBRASKA**
Omaha
Lincoln

**ILLINOIS**
Springfield
Chicago

**INDIANA**
Indianapolis

**OHIO**
Columbus
Cleveland
Cincinnati

**PENNSYLVANIA**
Harrisburg
Pittsburgh
Newark
New York

Trenton
Philadelphia

**NEW JERSEY**

Baltimore
Dover
Annapolis
Washington, D.C.

**DELAWARE**
**MARYLAND**

**KANSAS**
Kansas City
Topeka
Jefferson City

Kansas City

**MISSOURI**
St. Louis

Louisville

**KENTUCKY**
Frankfort

Ohio R.

**WEST VIRGINIA**
Charleston

**VIRGINIA**
Richmond
Norfolk

Missouri R.

Tulsa
Oklahoma City

**OKLAHOMA**

Fort Smith

**ARKANSAS**
Little Rock

Memphis

**TENNESSEE**
Nashville

**NORTH CAROLINA**
Greensboro
Raleigh

Mississippi River

**TEXAS**
Dallas
Austin
Houston
San Antonio

**LOUISIANA**
Baton Rouge
New Orleans

**MISSISSIPPI**
Jackson

Birmingham
Montgomery

**ALABAMA**
Mobile

**GEORGIA**
Atlanta
Savannah

**SOUTH CAROLINA**
Columbia
Charleston

Jacksonville
Tallahassee

**FLORIDA**
Tampa
Miami

**ATLANTIC OCEAN**

**Gulf of Mexico**

**BAHAMAS**

**CUBA**

Atlas

km 0  100  200  300  400  500
mi 0  100  200  300  400  500

R9

# United States: Physical

## Alaska Inset

ARCTIC OCEAN

70N

RUSSIA

Brooks Range

Bering Strait

Yukon R.

CANADA

Mt. McKinley
(Denali)
20,320 ft. ▲ Alaska Range

60N

Bering
Sea

170W

Gulf of
Alaska

Aleutian
Islands

Kodiak Is.

km 0    250   500

mi 0    250   500

160W        150W        140W

## Main Map

Mt. Rainier
14,410 ft.

Columbia R.

COAST RANGE

CASCADE RANGE

COLUMBIA PLATEAU

BITTERROOT RANGE

Missouri River

Yellowstone River

Mt. Hood
11,239 ft. ▲

ROCKY MOUNTAINS

BIGHORN MTNS.

GREAT

Black
Hills

Badlands

Snake River

Mt. Shasta
14,162 ft. ▲

Sacramento R.

SIERRA NEVADA

CENTRAL VALLEY

San Joaquin R.

BASIN
AND
RANGE

WASATCH RANGE

Green River

P
L
A
I
N
S

35N

San Francisco
Bay

Mt. Whitney
14,494 ft. ▲

Death Valley
282 ft. below sea level

Grand
Canyon

Painted
Desert

Colorado
Plateau

Colorado River

Pikes Peak
14,110 ft. ▲

SANGRE DE CRISTO MTNS.

PACIFIC
OCEAN

Mojave
Desert

CONTINENTAL DIVIDE

Channel Islands

30N

Gila River

Sonoran
Desert

Llano
Estacado

### LEGEND

15,000 ft. (4,500 m)
6,560 ft. (2,000 m)
3,280 ft. (1,000 m)
1,640 ft. (500 m)
650 ft. (200 m)
0 ft. (0 m)
Below sea level

▲ Highest Point

25N

Rio Grande

Pecos River

Edward
Plateau

MEXICO

Gulf of California

## Hawaii Inset

160W        155W

Kauai

Niihau        Oahu

Molokai

Lanai        Maui

Kahoolawe

Mauna Kea
13,796 ft. ▲

Hawaii

20N

PACIFIC OCEAN

Mauna Loa ▲
13,678 ft.

km 0   50   100

mi 0   50   100

Tropic of Cancer

115W        110W        105W

110W

CANADA

Mesabi Range

Lake Superior

St. Lawrence River

Mt. Washington 6,288 ft.

White Mtns.

Adirondack Mountains

Connecticut R.

Lake Michigan

Lake Huron

L. Ontario

ALLEGHENY PLATEAU

Catskill Mtns.

Hudson R.

Nantucket

Martha's Vineyard

Long Island

Sand Hills

Mississippi River

Lake Erie

Delaware River

Susquehanna River

Platte River

Des Moines River

Missouri River

CENTRAL PLAINS

Ohio R.

Delaware Bay

Chesapeake Bay

35N

OZARK PLATEAU

Arkansas River

Mississippi River

Cumberland Plateau

Mt. Mitchell 6,684 ft.

Tennessee R.

APPALACHIAN MOUNTAINS

BLUE RIDGE MOUNTAINS

FALL LINE

ATLANTIC COASTAL PLAIN

ATLANTIC OCEAN

OUACHITA MOUNTAINS

Red River

Wabash River

Savannah R.

Oconee R.

Chattahoochee River

Altamaha R.

30N

Sabine River

Tombigbee R.

Alabama R.

Brazos River

Colorado River

GULF

COASTAL

PLAIN

Pearl River

Mobile Bay

Pensacola Bay

Galveston Bay

Tampa Bay

25N

Gulf of Mexico

Everglades

BAHAMAS

Florida Keys

km 0 100 200 300 400 500

mi 0 100 200 300 400 500

Tropic of Cancer

95W        90W        85W

CUBA

75W

R11

## Africa: Political

ATLAS

EUROPE

ATLANTIC OCEAN

ASIA

Mediterranean Sea

Suez Canal

Algiers

Tunis

**TUNISIA**

Tripoli

Rabat

Canary Islands (Spain)

**MOROCCO**

Cairo

Nile River

**ALGERIA**

**LIBYA**

**EGYPT**

Red Sea

**WESTERN SAHARA (Morocco)**

Gulf of Aden

**CAPE VERDE**

**MAURITANIA**

**MALI**

Nouakchott

Niger R.

**NIGER**

**CHAD**

Khartoum

**ERITREA**

Asmara

**DJIBOUTI**

Djibouti

Praia

**SENEGAL**

Dakar

**GAMBIA**

Banjul

Bamako

**BURKINA FASO**

Niamey

Lake Chad

**SUDAN**

Addis Ababa

**SOMALIA**

**GUINEA-BISSAU**

Bissau

**GUINEA**

Ouagadougou

N'Djamena

**CENTRAL AFRICAN REPUBLIC**

**ETHIOPIA**

Conakry

**GHANA**

**BENIN**

**NIGERIA**

**SIERRA LEONE**

Freetown

**TOGO**

Abuja

Yamoussoukro

Accra

Porto-Novo

Bangui

**UGANDA**

**KENYA**

Mogadishu

Monrovia

Lomé

**CAMEROON**

**LIBERIA**

**CÔTE D'IVOIRE**

Gulf of Guinea

Malabo

Yaounde

Congo R.

Kampala

Lake Victoria

Nairobi

**EQUATORIAL GUINEA**

**SÃO TOMÉ & PRÍNCIPE**

São Tomé

Libreville

**REPUBLIC OF THE CONGO**

**RWANDA**

Kigali

**BURUNDI**

Bujumbura

**SEYCHELLES**

Victoria

**GABON**

Brazzaville

Kinshasa

**DEMOCRATIC REPUBLIC OF THE CONGO**

Lake Tanganyika

**TANZANIA**

Dar es Salaam

Ascension Island (U.K.)

**CABINDA (Angola)**

Luanda

**COMOROS**

Moroni

Mayotte (France)

N

W    E

S

**ANGOLA**

Lake Malawi

**MALAWI**

Lilongwe

Antananarivo

Port Louis

St. Helena Island (U.K.)

**ZAMBIA**

Lusaka

**MOZAMBIQUE**

Mozambique Channel

**MADAGASCAR**

Réunion (France)

Harare

**NAMIBIA**

**ZIMBABWE**

**MAURITIUS**

Windhoek

**BOTSWANA**

Gaborone

Pretoria

Maputo

Mbabane

**SWAZILAND**

ATLANTIC OCEAN

Maseru

**SOUTH AFRICA**

**LESOTHO**

Cape Town

INDIAN OCEAN

**KEY**

⊛  National capital

—  National border

km 0    500    1,000

mi 0    500    1,000

## Africa: Physical

ATLANTIC OCEAN

EUROPE

ASIA

ATLAS MOUNTAINS

Mt. Toubkal

Canary Islands

Mediterranean Sea

Suez Canal

Nile River

Lake Nasser

Red Sea

AHAGGAR MOUNTAINS

TIBESTI MTS.

Libyan Desert

Nubian Desert

S A H A R A

Niger River

Lake Chad

Chari River

FOUTA DJALLON MTS.

Benue River

Lake Volta

White Nile

Blue Nile

Gulf of Aden

ETHIOPIAN HIGHLANDS

Mt. Cameroon

Bioko

Gulf of Guinea

Uele River

Congo River

Lake Turkana

Margherita Peak

Lake Victoria

Mt. Kenya

Ascension Island

CONGO BASIN

MITUMBA MTS.

Serengeti Plain

Mt. Kilimanjaro

Pemba Island

Zanzibar Island

L. Tanganyika

GREAT RIFT VALLEY

N
W     E
S

Katanga Plateau

Comoros Islands

St. Helena Island

Bié Plateau

Lake Malawi

Mayotte

Zambezi R.

Victoria Falls

Lake Kariba

Madagascar

ATLANTIC OCEAN

Namib Desert

Limpopo R.

Mozambique Channel

Réunion

Kalahari Desert

Orange R.

DRAKENSBERG MOUNTAINS

INDIAN OCEAN

### KEY

7,000 ft. (2,133 m)
3,750 ft. (1,143 m)
2,075 ft. (632 m)
1,200 ft. (366 m)
600 ft. (183 m)
0 ft. (0 m)
Below sea level

▲ Highest peak

▲ Mountain

km 0    500    1,000
mi 0    500    1,000

## Asia: Political

ARCTIC OCEAN

EUROPE

RUSSIA

• Moscow

• Yekaterinburg

• Chelyabinsk

• Novosibirsk

Laptev Sea

Lena River

Ob River

Lake Baikal

Ulaanbaatar ⊛

MONGOLIA

Astana ⊛

KAZAKHSTAN

• Karaganda

Aral Sea

Lake Balkhash

Istanbul

Black Sea

Caspian Sea

Izmir

Ankara ⊛

GEORGIA

Tbilisi ⊛

TURKEY

ARMENIA

Yerevan ⊛

AZERBAIJAN

Baku •

Nicosia ⊛

CYPRUS

LEBANON

Beirut ⊛

Jerusalem ⊛

SYRIA

Damascus •

ISRAEL

Amman •

JORDAN

Baghdad •

IRAQ

TURKMENISTAN

Ashgabat ⊛

UZBEKISTAN

Tashkent •

Bishkek ⊛

Almaty •

KYRGYZSTAN

Dushanbe ⊛

TAJIKISTAN

CHINA

Tehran •

Mashhad •

IRAN

AFGHANISTAN

Kabul •

Huang He

Taiyua

Xi'an •

Kuwait •

KUWAIT

BAHRAIN

Manama ⊛

Riyadh ⊛

Doha •

QATAR

Abu Dhabi •

U.A.E.

Muscat ⊛

Islamabad ⊛

Lahore •

PAKISTAN

Indus R.

Delhi •

New Delhi •

Kanpur •

Ganges R.

NEPAL

Kathmandu ⊛

Chengdu •

Mekong R.

Chang Jiang (Yangtze R.)

Thimphu ⊛

BHUTAN

Persian Gulf

Red Sea

SAUDI ARABIA

OMAN

Sanaa ⊛

YEMEN

Ahmadabad •

BANGLADESH

Kolkata •

Dhaka ⊛

VIETNAM

Hanoi •

MYANMAR (BURMA)

LAOS

Vientiane ⊛

INDIA

Nagpur •

Naypyidaw •

Arabian Sea

Gulf of Aden

AFRICA

Mumbai •

Bangalore •

Chennai •

Bay of Bengal

Yangon (Rangoon) •

THAILAND

Bangkok ⊛

CAMBODIA

Phn

INDIAN OCEAN

MALDIVES

Male •

Colombo ⊛

SRI LANKA

Medan •

MALAYS

Kuala Lum ⊛

Singa •

SINGAPORE

N

W    E

S

Jakarta •

Bandun

East
Siberian
Sea

Bering Sea

Aleutian Islands
(U.S.)

Sea of
Okhotsk

Sakhalin

Kuril Islands

**KEY**

⊛ National capital

• Major city

— National border

Heilong River

Harbin

East
Sea

JAPAN

Changchun

**NORTH
KOREA**

⊛ P'yongyang

⊛ Tokyo

Nagoya

⊛ Beijing

⊛ Seoul

Osaka

Tianjin

**SOUTH
KOREA**

• Pusan

iyuan

Jinan

Nanjing

Shanghai

Wuhan

East
China
Sea

Ryukyu Islands
(Japan)

R.)

Taipei

**TAIWAN**

Kaohsiung

Hong Kong

Philippine
Sea

**NAM**

South
China
Sea

Manila

iane

**PHILIPPINES**

**ODIA**

Phnom Penh

Ho Chi Minh City

Bandar Seri Begawan

**AYSIA**

Celebes Sea

⊛ **BRUNEI**

a Lumpur

Singapore

**APORE**

**I N D O N E S I A**

Banda Sea

Java
Sea

akarta

Surabaya

**EAST TIMOR**

Bandung

Dili

**PACIFIC
OCEAN**

km 0    400    800

mi 0         400    800

R15

Asia: Physical

ARCTIC OCEAN

EUROPE

URAL MOUNTAINS

Ob River

Ob River

Lena River

Lena River

Irtysh River

Lake Baikal

Black Sea

CAUCASUS

Aras R.

Caspian Sea

Aral Sea

Lake Balkhash

Cyprus

Mediterranean Sea

Amy Darya River

Syr Darya R.

GOBI DESERT

Euphrates River

Tigris River

Huang He

Persian Gulf

Indus River

HIMALAYAS

Brahmaputra R.

Mt. Everest

Chang Jiang (Yangtze R.)

Salween R.

Arabian Peninsula

Ganges R.

Red River

Arabian Sea

Godavari River

Mekong R.

AFRICA

Indian Peninsula

Bay of Bengal

INDIAN OCEAN

Gulf of Thailand

Malay Peninsula

N
W    E
S

Sumatra

Indigirka R.

Kolyma R.

Aleutian Islands

Sakhalin

Heilong R.

Kuril Islands

Korean
Peninsula

Japanese Archipelago

KEY

4,000 ft. (1,219 m)
2,000 ft. (609 m)
1,000 ft. (305 m)
500 ft. (152 m)
250 ft. (76 m)
0 ft. (0 m)
Below sea level

▲  Highest point

km 0    400    800
mi 0    400    800

PACIFIC
OCEAN

T

Riukyu Islands

Yangtze R.)

River

Mekong R.

Philippine Archipelago

South
China
Sea

Celebes
Sea

Borneo

matra

Indonesian  Archipelago

**R17**

Atlas

ICELAND
⭐ Reykjavík

ATLANTIC
OCEAN

Norwegian
Sea

Faroe Islands
(Denmark)

Shetland
Islands
(U.K.)

N
W   E
S

SWEDEN

FINLAND

NORWAY

⭐ Oslo

Lake
Onega

RUSSI

Lake
Ladoga

Rybinsk
Reservoir

Volg

⭐ Helsinki

Stockholm
⭐

Tallinn
⭐

ESTONIA

Lake
Vänern

Baltic Sea

Moscow
⭐

Riga
⭐
LATVIA

LITHUANIA
Vilnius
⭐

Minsk
⭐

BELARUS

KALININGRAD
(Rus.)

SCOTLAND

NORTHERN
IRELAND

North
Sea

DENMARK
Copenhagen ⭐

Dublin
⭐
UNITED
KINGDOM

IRELAND

ENGLAND

WALES

London
⭐

Thames R.

English Channel

NETHERLANDS
⭐ Amsterdam

The Hague ⭐

Brussels ⭐
BELGIUM
LUXEMBOURG

Rhine R.

Berlin
⭐

GERMANY

Warsaw
⭐

POLAND

Kiev ⭐

UKRAINE

⭐ Luxembourg

Seine River

⭐ Paris

FRANCE

Bern
⭐
SWITZERLAND

Vaduz
⭐
LIECHTENSTEIN

⭐ Prague

CZECH REP.

SLOVAKIA

Bratislava
⭐

Vienna
⭐
AUSTRIA

⭐ Budapest

HUNGARY

MOLDOVA

Chisinau
⭐

ROMANIA

Bucharest
⭐

SLOVENIA
Ljubljana ⭐

ITALY

Zagreb
⭐
CROATIA

Belgrade
⭐

Danube R.

Black
Sea

MONACO ⭐

ANDORRA

Andorra la Vella
⭐

PORTUGAL

Madrid
⭐

⭐ Lisbon

SPAIN

SAN
MARINO
⭐

Adriatic Sea

BOSNIA &
HERZEGOVINA

Sarajevo
⭐

MONTENEGRO

SERBIA

Podgorica
⭐

Pristina
⭐
KOSOVO

Skopje
⭐
MACEDONIA

Sofia
⭐

BULGARIA

TURKEY

VATICAN
CITY
⭐

Rome
⭐

Tirana
⭐
ALBANIA

GREECE

Aegean
Sea

Athens
⭐

An

Tyrrhenian
Sea

Ionian
Sea

⭐ Valletta

MALTA

Sea

AFRICA

Mediterranean

Strait of
Gibraltar

Area of detail

Detail

POLAND

UKRAINE

⊛ Prague

CZECH REP.

SLOVAKIA

MOLDOVA

Bratislava

⊛ Chisinau

Vienna ⊛

⊛ Budapest

RUSSIA

AUSTRIA

HUNGARY

ROMANIA

SLOVENIA

Zagreb ⊛

Bucharest

Ljubljana ⊛

CROATIA

Belgrade ⊛

⊛

BOSNIA &

HERZEGOVINA

SERBIA

BULGARIA

SAN

MARINO

Sarajevo ⊛

Danube R.

Black

Sea

MONTENEGRO

Pristina ⊛

⊛ ⊛

Sofia

VATICAN

CITY

Podgorica ⊛

KOSOVO

⊛ Skopje

TURKEY

MACEDONIA

Rome ⊛

Tirana ⊛ ⊛

Aegean

Sea

ITALY

ALBANIA

GREECE

Tyrrhenian

Sea

Ionian

Sea

⊛ Athens

Mediterranean Sea

MALTA ⊛ Valletta

km 0      200    400

mi  0           200          400

RUSSIA

⊛IA

Volga River

KAZAKHSTAN

ASIA

Volga River

Caspian Sea

GEORGIA

⊛ Baku

Tbilisi ⊛

Black

Sea

AZERBAIJAN

Y ⊛

Ankara ⊛

KEY

⊛   National capital

———  National border

km 0      200    400

mi  0           200          400

Atlas

Barents Sea

Iceland

Norwegian
Sea

N
W          E
S

Faroe
Islands

ATLANTIC
OCEAN

Shetland
Islands

KJOLEN

SCANDINAVIAN SHIELD

Gulf of Bothnia

Lake
Saimaa

Lake
Onega

Lake
Ladoga

Volg

Rybinsk
Reservoir

Lake
Peipus

Lake
Vänern

Hebrides

North
Sea

Lough
Neagh

Shannon
River

PENNINES

Lake
Vättern

Gotland

Baltic Sea

NORTH EUROPEAN PLAIN

Dnieper River

Thames R.

English Channel

Channel Islands

Elbe River

Oder River

Vistula River

Rhine River

CARPATHIAN MTS.

Seine River

Bay of
Biscay

Loire River

Lake
Geneva

Lake

ALPS

MASSIF
CENTRAL

Po River

Lake
Balaton

GREAT
HUNGARIAN
PLAIN

Danube River

Black
Sea

PYRENEES

Arno R.

Corsica

APENNINES

Adriatic Sea

BALKAN MTS.

MESETA

Sardinia

Tiber R.

Tyrrhenian
Sea

Ionian
Sea

Aegean
Sea

Balearic
Islands

Mediterranean

Sicily

Strait of
Gibraltar

AFRICA

Malta

Crete

Sea

Area of detail

URAL MOUNTAINS

Volga River

Don River

Caspian Sea

CAUCASUS MTS.

Black Sea

ASIA

**Detail**

CARPATHIAN MTS.

Danube R.

Prut R.

GREAT HUNGARIAN PLAIN

ALPS

Tisza R.

Danube R.

Black Sea

BALKAN MTS.

BALKAN PENINSULA

APENNINES

Adriatic Sea

Aegean Sea

Tyrrhenian Sea

Ionian Sea

Peloponnesus

Sicily

Crete

Mediterranean Sea

| km 0 | 200 | 400 |
| --- | --- | --- |
| mi 0 | 200 | 400 |

**KEY**

5,500 ft. (1,676 m)
2,250 ft. (686 m)
1,250 ft. (381 m)
550 ft. (168 m)
275 ft. (84 m)
0 ft. (0 m)
Below sea level

| km 0 | 200 | 400 |
| --- | --- | --- |
| mi 0 | 200 | 400 |

# South America: Political

Caribbean Sea

ATLANTIC OCEAN

Panama Canal

Maracaibo

Lake Maracaibo

⊛ Caracas

**VENEZUELA**

Georgetown ⊛
**GUYANA**
Paramaribo
**SURINAME**
**FRENCH GUIANA (Fr.)**

• Medellín
⊛ Bogotá
**COLOMBIA**
• Cali

⊛ Quito
**ECUADOR**
• Guayaquil

Galápagos Islands (Ecuador)

**PERU**

Amazon River

Manaus •
• Belém

**BRAZIL**

• Recife

⊛ Lima

Lake Titicaca
⊛ La Paz
**BOLIVIA**
• Sucre

Brasília ⊛

Salvador •

**PARAGUAY**

Paraná River

Belo Horizonte •

São Paulo •
Curitiba •

Rio de Janeiro •

N
W     E
S

PACIFIC OCEAN

Asunción ⊛

**CHILE**

**ARGENTINA**

Porto Alegre •

**URUGUAY**

• Córdoba

Rosario •

⊛ Montevideo

Buenos Aires ⊛

Río de la Plata

Santiago ⊛

## KEY
- ⊛ National capital
- • Major city
- — National border

ATLANTIC OCEAN

km 0 — 400 — 800
mi 0 — 400 — 800

Falkland Islands (U.K.)

Strait of Magellan

South Georgia (U.K.)

Atlas

South America: Physical

Caribbean Sea

ATLANTIC OCEAN

Atlas

Panama Canal

Lake Maracaibo

Orinoco River

L L A N O S

Angel Falls

Casiquiare River

Magdalena River

A M A Z O N

Galápagos Islands

Guayas River

Amazon River

Marañón River

B A S I N

São Francisco River

Ucayali River

A N D E S

Santa River
Lake Junin

Lake Saracocha

Lake Titicaca

Lake Poopó

BRAZILIAN

HIGHLANDS

N
W    E
S

Paraguay River

PACIFIC OCEAN

Atacama Desert

A N D E S

Paraná

River

Patos Lagoon

Mt. Aconcagua

P A M P A S

Paraná

Rio de la Plata

**KEY**

4,500 ft. (1,372 m)
2,000 ft. (610 m)
1,000 ft. (305 m)
500 ft. (152 m)
200 ft. (61 m)
0 ft. (0 m)
Below sea level

▲ Highest peak

〓 Waterfall

Lake
Nahuel
Huapi

ATLANTIC OCEAN

Lake
Buenos
Aires

Patagonia

km 0    400    800

mi 0    400    800

Lake Argentino

Strait of Magellan

Falkland Islands

South Georgia

Scotia Sea

R23

# Glossary

**adapt** (uh DAPT) to change to fit a new place or event. (p. 13)

**agriculture** (AG rih kul chur) the growing of crops and the raising of animals. (p. 29)

**ancestor** (AN sehs tuhr) someone in your family who lived long before you. (p. 123)

**archipelago** (ahr kih PEHL uh goh) a large group of islands. (p. 99)

**architecture** (AHR kih tehk chuhr) the design of buildings and other structures. (p. 161)

**artifact** (AHR ti fakt) an object that tells us about the culture of the people who made it. (p. 66)

**artisan** (AHR tih zuhn) a skilled worker who makes goods by hand. (p. 76)

**bar graph** (bahr graf) a graph with bar shapes for comparing amounts of things. (p. 102)

**bay** (bay) part of an ocean or lake that extends into the land. (p. 200)

**calligraphy** (kah LIHG rah fee) the art of writing characters with brushes and ink. (p. 124)

**canal** (kuh NAL) a waterway made by people. (p. 50)

**capital** (KAP ih tuhl) the city where a state or country's government is located. (p. 70)

**capital resources** (KAP ih tuhl REE sawrs ehz) things used by people to make goods or provide services. (p. 17)

**cardinal directions** (KAR duh nuhl dih REK shunz) the main directions: north, south, east, and west. (p. 14)

**century** (SEHN chuh ree) a period of 100 years. (p. 64)

**civilization** (sihv uh lih ZAY shuhn) a group of people who live together with a shared culture, including writing, agriculture, science, and art. (p. 29)

**claim** (klaym) to say that you own something, such as a piece of land. (p. 209)

**climate** (KLY miht) the weather of a place over a long period of time. (p. 12)

**coastline** (KOHST liyn) the shape or outline of land where it meets the ocean. (p. 147)

**colony** (KAHL uh nee) an area under another country's control. (p. 68)

**command economy** (kuh MAND ih KAHN uh mee) a system in which the government decides what to make and who will make it. (p. 106)

**communist** (KAHM yuh nihst) someone who believes the government should own a country's resources and decide how to divide them among the people. (p. 114)

**compass** (KUHM puhs) a tool used to figure out geographic direction. (p. 113)

**compass rose** (KUHM puhs ROHZ) a symbol that shows directions on a map. (p. 14)

**compromise** (KAHM pruh myz) a plan that everyone agrees on. (p. 168)

**constitution** (kahn stih TOO shuhn) a written plan for a country's government. (p. 164)

**consumer** (kuhn SOO muhr) a person who buys or uses a product. (p. 154)

**continent** (KAHN tuh nuhnt) one of seven large land areas on Earth. (p. 9)

**culture** (KUHL chuhr) the way of life a group of people share. (p. 22)

**decade** (DEHK ayd) a period of ten years. (p. 64)

**delta** (DEHL tah) a triangle of sand and soil deposited by a river. (p. 56)

**democracy** (dih MAHK ruh see) a form of government in which the people make the decisions about how they should be ruled. (p. 32)

**diversity** (dih VUR sih tee) variety or differences. (p. 74)

**dynasty** (DYH nuh stee) a series of rulers from the same family. (p. 112)

**economy** (ih KAHN uh mee) the way that people choose to make, buy, sell, and use things. (p. 31)

**elder** (EHL duhr) an older person, such as a grandparent. (p. 123)

**elevation** (ehl eh VAY shuhn) how high above sea level a place is. (p. 196)

**empire** (EHM pyr) a group of nations ruled by one government. (p. 161)

**endangered** (ehn DAYN jehrd) when a plant or an animal is in danger of dying out. (p. 52)

**environment** (ehn VY ruhn muhnt) the water, soil, air, and living things around you. (p. 16)

**equator** (ih KWAY tuhr) a line of latitude that circles the globe exactly halfway between the North and South poles. (p. 198)

**ethnic group** (EHTH nihk groop) a group of people who have their own language and culture. (p. 25)

**export** (EHK spawrt) a good shipped and sold to another country. (p. 108)

**extended family** (ehk STEN dehd FAM ih lee) members of a family that includes grandparents, aunts, uncles, cousins, and others. (p. 219)

**festival** (FEHS tih vuhl) a special event where people celebrate the arts. (p. 172)

**fjord** (fyohrd) a long, deep, narrow part of the sea that cuts into the land and runs between cliffs. (p. 146)

**folktale** (FOHK tayl) a story passed from one generation to the next. (p. 76)

**geography** (jee AHG ruh fee) the study of people, places, and Earth. (p. 10)

**glacier** (GLAY shur) a huge mass of slow-moving ice. (p. 194)

**government** (GUHV uhrn muhnt) the group of people that makes laws and keeps order. (p. 32)

**hemisphere** (HEHM ih sfihr) one half of Earth's surface. (p. 198)

**heritage** (HEHR ih tihj) the history, ideas, and beliefs that people receive from the past. (p. 75)

**high-tech** (hy TEHK) using advanced scientific knowledge to get work done. (p. 202)

**human resources** (HYOO muhn REE sawrs ehz) the skills, knowledge, and hard work that people bring to their jobs. (p. 17)

**hunter-gatherer** (HUN tuhr GA thuh ruhr) a person who hunts animals and gathers plants for food. (p. 208)

**hydroelectric power** (hy droh ih LEHK trihk powh uhr) electricity created by moving water. (p. 201)

**immigration** (ihm ih GRAY shuhn) moving to a new country. (p. 218)

**import** (IHM pawrt) a good that is bought from another country. (p. 108)

**independence** (IHN dih pehn duhns) freedom from someone else's control. (p. 69)

**industry** (IHN duh stree) all the companies and people that make or sell one kind of product or service. (p. 58)

**intermediate directions** (ihn tuhr MEE dee iht dih REK shunz) directions that fall between the cardinal directions: northeast, northwest, southeast, southwest. (p. 14)

**Internet** (IHN tuhr neht) a large system of computer networks. (p. 150)

**irrigation** (ihr ih GAY shuhn) bringing water to dry places. (p. 105)

**landform** (LAND fohrm) a shape or feature on the Earth's surface. (p. 9)

**latitude** (LAT ih tood) lines that cross the globe from side to side. (p. 198)

**leisure time** (LEE zhuhr tym) free time. (p. 222)

**longitude** (LAHN jih tood) lines that cross the globe from top to bottom. (p. 198)

**manufacturing** (man yuh FAK chur ing) the making of products with machines. (p. 58)

**map key** (map kee) information that tells what the colors, pictures, and lines on a map mean. (p. 14)

**map scale** (map skayl) symbols that help measure distances on a map. (p. 54)

**map title** (map TY tuhl) information that tells what is shown on a map. (p. 14)

**market economy** (MAHR kiht ih KAHN uh mee) a system in which individuals, not the government, decide what jobs they will have. (p. 154)

**martial art** (MAHR shuhl ahrt) the art of using the body for self-defense. (p. 124)

**millennium** (muh LEHN ee uhm) a period of 1,000 years. (p. 64)

**moderate** (MAH dehr eht) mild. (p. 148)

**modernize** (MAH dehr nyz) to make something up-to-date. (p. 210)

**monarchy** (MAHN ahr kee) a country ruled by a king or queen. (p. 210)

**monsoon** (mahn SOON) a system of winds that may bring heavy rain at certain seasons. (p. 100)

**natural resources** (NACH ur uhl REE sawrs ehz) things found in nature that are useful to people. (p. 16)

**needs** (needz) things people must have in order to live. (p. 24)

**opera** (AH puh rhah) a play in which most of the words are sung and accompanied by an orchestra. (p. 172)

**peninsula** (puh NIHN suh luh) land nearly surrounded by water. (p. 99)

**point of view** (poynt uhv vyoo) the way a person thinks about an issue. (p. 216)

**pollution** (puh LOO shuhn) anything that makes the environment dirty or harmful. (p. 106)

**popular music** (PAHP yuh luhr MYOO zik) tunes and songs that many people enjoy listening to. (p. 220)

**population** (pahp yuh LAY shun) the number of people who live in a place. (p. 170)

**primary source** (PRY mehr ee sawrs) something created by a person who was there. (p. 120)

**prime meridian** (prym muh RIHD ee uhn) a line of longitude that passes through Greenwich, England. (p. 198)

**producer** (pruh DOO suhr) someone who makes and sells goods. (p. 154)

**rain forest** (rayn FOHR ihst) a forest that has many trees and lots of rain. (p. 51)

**reference book** (REHF uhr uhns buk) a book that contains facts on different subjects. (p. 150)

**region** (REE juhn) an area that shares one or more features. (p. 18)

**Renaissance** (rehn ih SAHNS) a time of major change in art and science across Europe. (p. 162)

**republic** (rih PUHB lik) a form of government with elected leaders. (p. 114)

**rural** (RUR uhl) an area far from the city, with open spaces. (p. 60)

**savanna** (suh VAN nah) land with tall grass and few trees. (p. 51)

**secondary source** (SEHK uhn dehr ee sawrs) something created by a person who was not there. (p. 120)

**slavery** (SLAY vuh ree) a cruel system
in which people have no freedom and
are forced to work without pay. (p. 68)

**steppe** (stehp) a large grassy plain.
(p. 98)

**strait** (strayt) a narrow waterway that
connects two big bodies of water.
(p. 195)

**timeline** (TYM lyn) something that
shows the dates of events and the
order in which they occur. (p. 64)

**tourism** (TUHR ism) traveling for fun.
(p. 156)

**tradition** (truh DIH shuhn) a culture's
special way of doing things. (p. 23)

**tributary** (TRIH byuh tayr ee) a smaller
river that flows into a larger one.
(p. 194)

**tundra** (TUHN drah) a cold, treeless
land area. (p. 97)

**urban** (UR buhn) having to do with a
city. (p. 60)

# Index

Page numbers with *m* before them refer to maps.

**A**

**Abuja, Nigeria,** *m59*, 70
**Aconcagua, Mount,** *m2*, *m195*
**Adapt,** 13
**Ade, King Sunny,** 77
**Africa,** 49–53
  Africa Cup winners, 43
  bodies of water, 45, 49, 50
  cities, 45, *m55*
  climate, 52
  Kalahari Desert, 51
  Kilimanjaro, Mount, *m3*, 49, *m51*
  Lagos, 45, *m58*
  landforms, 49, *m50*
  Namib Desert, 51
  natural resources, 53
  Nigeria, 56–60, 62–63, 66–70, 74–78, 80–81
  Nile River, 49, 50
  physical map, *mR13*
  political map, *m42*, *mR12*
  population in, 43
  rain forests, 51
  regions, 50, 56
  rivers and lakes, 45, 49, 50
  Sahara, 49, 51
  Savanna, 51, 52
  vegetation, 51, 52
  wildlife, 52
**Africans, in Brazil,** 218
**Agriculture,** 29. *See also* Farming.
**Alcântara,** 206
**Alps,** 137, 146, *m147*, 152, *m153*, 156
**Amalfi Coast, Italy,** 156
**Amaral, Tarsila do,** 221
**Amazon Rain Forest,** *m195*, 202, 214–215, 226–227
**Amazon River,** 193, 194, 195, 214–215, 226–227
**Amazon River Basin,** 194, *m201*, 206
**Ancestor,** 123, 193, 218
**Ancient Rome,** 141, 160–161, 165, 166–167
**Andes,** 194, *m195*, 196
**Andrade, Mário de,** 220
**Apennine Mountains,** 152, *m153*
**Arabian Peninsula,** *m99*

**Archipelago,** 99
**Architecture,** 143, 161
  in ancient Rome, 161, 165, 166–167
  in Brasília, 211, 213
  in China, 113, 117
**Arctic Ocean,** 147
**Argungu Fishing Festival,** 81
**Art,** 72–73, 76, 124, 162, 172
**Artifact,** 47, 66
**Artisan,** 47, 76
**Asia,** 97
  Arabian Peninsula, *m99*
  bodies of water, 99
  Caucasus Mountains, 98
  China, 104–108, 110–111, 112–116, 122–126, 128–129
  climate, 100
  earthquakes, 92–93
  Gobi Desert, 98, 104
  Himalayas, 98
  Indian Ocean, *m99*
  Indian Peninsula, 99
  islands, 98, 99
  Korean Peninsula, *m99*
  landforms, 98, *m99*
  Malay Peninsula, *m99*
  Mumbai, India, 97
  natural resources, 100
  Pacific Ocean, 99
  physical map, *mR16*
  political map, *m90*, *mR18*
  populations, 91, 97
  regions, 98–101
  Ring of Fire, 93
  Tokyo, Japan, 97
  vegetation, 101
  volcanoes, 93
  wildlife, 101
**Atacama Desert,** 194
**Atlantic Ocean,** 18, 147, 195
**Atlas,** *mR4–mR23*

**Ban Zhao,** 120
**Bargnani, Andrea,** 179
**Bar graph,** 102
**Bari, Italy,** *m155*
**Basin,** 195
**Bay,** 200
**Beijing, China,** *m107*
**Belmondo, Stefania,** 179
**Benin, Kingdom of,** 67, *m67*, 72–73
**Benue River,** *m57*

**Biography Features**
  Bargnani, Andrea, 179
  Belmondo, Stefania, 179
  Cannavaro, Fabio, 178
  Douglas, Marjory Stoneman, 21
  Empress Lü, 119
  Fu Hao, 118
  Muir, John, 20
  Silva, Marina, 226–227
  Soyinka, Wole, 82–83
**Bocce,** 174
**Bossa nova,** 220
**Botany,** 20
**Brasília,** *m203*, 211, 212
**Brazil,** *m201*
  Alcântara, 206
  Amazon rain forest, *m195*, 202, 214–215, 226–227
  bodies of water, 200–201, 214–215
  celebrations and holidays, 203, 225
  climate, 201
  culture, 218, 219, 224–225
  current issues and problems, 212
  economy, 200, 202, 203
  flag, 224
  Golden Law, 210
  government, 208, 211, 212
  history, 208–211
  holidays, 225
  jobs in, *m202–203*
  land, 200
  landforms, 200, *m201*
  location, 200
  Pedro I, 210
  Pedro II, 210
  people and groups, 208, 210, 218
  products and industries, 201, 202, *m202–203*
  regions, 204
  religions of, 219
  resources, 201
  rural areas, 204
  school calendar, 222
  seal, 224
  Silva, Marina, 226–227
  symbols, 224
  urban areas, 204
  vegetation, 201, 214–215
  wildlife, 214
  Yanomami, 208
**Bronzino, Agnolo,** 173
**Buddhist, in Brazil,** 219

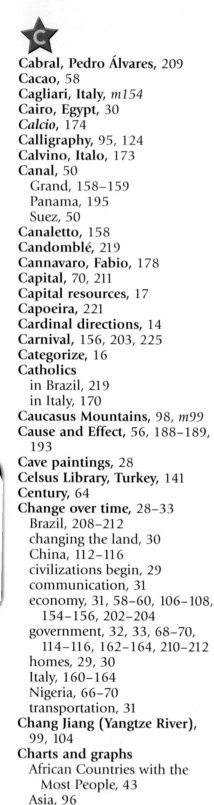

## C

Cabral, Pedro Álvares, 209
Cacao, 58
Cagliari, Italy, m154
Cairo, Egypt, 30
Calcio, 174
Calligraphy, 95, 124
Calvino, Italo, 173
Canal, 50
    Grand, 158–159
    Panama, 195
    Suez, 50
Canaletto, 158
Candomblé, 219
Cannavaro, Fabio, 178
Capital, 70, 211
Capital resources, 17
Capoeira, 221
Cardinal directions, 14
Carnival, 156, 203, 225
Categorize, 16
Catholics
    in Brazil, 219
    in Italy, 170
Caucasus Mountains, 98, m99
Cause and Effect, 56, 188–189, 193
Cave paintings, 28
Celsus Library, Turkey, 141
Century, 64
Change over time, 28–33
    Brazil, 208–212
    changing the land, 30
    China, 112–116
    civilizations begin, 29
    communication, 31
    economy, 31, 58–60, 106–108, 154–156, 202–204
    government, 32, 33, 68–70, 114–116, 162–164, 210–212
    homes, 29, 30
    Italy, 160–164
    Nigeria, 66–70
    transportation, 31
Chang Jiang (Yangtze River), 99, 104
Charts and graphs
    African Countries with the Most People, 43
    Asia, 96
    Asian Countries with the Most People, 91
    Asia's Internet Users, 91
    China's Government, Then and Now, 116
    China's Top Export Countries, 110
    Comparing Cultures, 24

Comparing Languages, 26
European Countries with the Most People, 139
Independent Countries of the World, 103
Italy's Leaders, 164
Large Cities in China, 135
Largest Groups in Nigeria, 75
Mountains Around the World, 3
Nigeria's Government, 70
Rivers Around the World, 3
School Calendar in Brazil, 222
South American Countries with the Most People, 187
South American Languages, 187
Top Winners of Africa Cup of Nations, 43
Visitors to Europe, 2004, 139
Voting in Brazil and the United States, 212
Chengdu, China, m107
Chiang Kai-shek, 114, 115
China
    bodies of water, 99, 104
    celebrations and holidays, 128–129
    Chiang Kai-shek, 114, 115
    climate, 105
    Communist Party, 114
    culture, 122–125, 128–129
    current issues and problems, 116
    Deng Xiaoping, 115
    economy, 104, 106–108
    Empress Lü, 119
    flag, 128
    Fu Hao, 118
    government, 112, 114–116
    Great Wall, 89, 112, 113
    Han dynasty, 122
    history, 112–115
    inventions, 113
    jobs in, m106–107
    land, 104, m107
    landforms, 104–105, m105
    leaders, timeline of, 114–115
    location, 104–105, 112
    Mao Zedong, 115, 116
    Nationalist Party, 114
    people and groups, 122
    People's Republic of China, 115
    population, 104, 122
    products and industries, 106, m106–107
    Qin dynasty, 112
    Qing dynasty, 114
    regions, 105

    resources, 104, 105, 107
    Shang dynasty, 112
    Sun Yat-sen, 114
    symbols, 128
Chinese New Year, 129
Christians, in Nigeria, 78, 80
Christmas, 78
Citizenship Skills
    Point of view, 216
    Resolve conflicts, 168
City-state, 162
Civilization, 29–30, 66–67, 72–73, 112–113, 160–161
Claim, 209
Climate, 6, 12
    Africa, 52
    Asia, 100
    Brazil, 201
    China, 105
    Europe, 148
    Italy, 153
    moderate, 148
    Nigeria, 57
    polar, 100
    South America, 196
    tropical, 52, 100, 196, 201
Coastline, 147, 201
Collodi, Carlo, 173
Colony, 68, 210
Colosseum, 160, 161
Command economy, 106
Communication, changes in, 31
Communist, 114–115
Compare and Contrast, 44–45, 49, 86, 159
Compass, 113
Compass rose, 14
Compromise, 168
Confucius, 130–131
Congo River, 50
Congolian Forests, m51
Constitution, xiv–xv, 164, 211
Constitution Day, xiv–xv
Consumer, 154
Continent, 9, 49, 97, 103, 145, 193
Cultural landscapes, 30
Culture, 22–25
    Brazil, 218–223, 224–225
    China, 122–127, 128–129
    comparing, 24
    heritage, 76
    Italy, 170–175, 176–177
    Nigeria, 74–79, 80–81
    mix of cultures, 25
    religion, 23
    sharing, 23
    traditions, 23

**Dance,** 81, 125, 172
**Decade,** 64
**Delta,** 56, 61
**Democracy,** 32, 69, 82, 211
**Deng Xiaoping,** 115
**Directions**
 cardinal, 14
 intermediate, 14
**Diversity,** 74, 122, 170, 218
**Douglas, Marjory Stoneman,** 21
**Dragon Boat Festival,** 129
**Dynasty,** 95, 112
 Han, 119
 Qin, 112
 Qing, 114
 Shang, 112

**Early people,** 28
**Ebony,** 53
**Economy,** 31
 Brazil, 202–204
 China, 106–108, 110–111
 Italy, 154–156
 Nigeria, 58–60
**Edo, Kingdom of,** 67
**Edwards, William H.,** 214
**Egungun Festival,** 78, 81
**Egypt,** 24, 30, 34–35, 43
**Egyptian Hieroglyphics,** 34–35
**Elder,** 123
**Elevation,** 196
*El Niño,* 188–189
**Empire,** 142, 161
**Empress Lü,** 119
**Endangered,** 46, 52, 101, 226
**England,** 147
**Environment,** 16, 51
**Equator,** 198, 201
**Ethnic groups,** 7, 25
 Asian, 122
 Chinese, 122
 Han, 122
 Hausa, 67, 75
 Igbo, 66, 75
 Nigerian, 66–67, 74–75
 Portuguese, 218
 South Americans, 193
 South American Indian, 193, 208, 218
 Yanomami, 208
 Yoruba, 67, 75
**Etna, Mount,** 156
**Euro,** 163
**Europe,** 145
 ancient Rome, 141

bodies of water, 147
climate, 148
euro, 163
European Union, 145
Italy, 152–157, 158–159, 160–165, 170–175, 176–177, 178–179
landforms, 145, 146, *m147*
most populous nations, 139
natural resources, 149
physical map, *mR20*
political map, *m138*, *mR18*
population graph, 139
regions, 148, 152
Southern Europe, 148, 152
tourism graph, 139
vegetation, 148, 149
Western Europe, 148
wildlife, 148
**European Union,** 145, 163
**Everest, Mount,** 97
**Everglades, Florida,** 21
**Export,** 94, 108, 153
**Extended family,** 191, 219

**Families,** 75, 123, 171, 191, 219
**Farming,** 29, 100, 106, 107, 154, 155, 202
**Festival,** 143, 195
**Festivals,** 172
 Argungu Fishing Festival, 81
 Carnival, 156, 225
 Dragon Boat Festival, 129
 Egungun Festival, 78, 81
 June Festivals, 225
 Lantern Festival, 129
 Osun Oshogbo, 81
**Fishing,** 81, 155
**Fjord,** 142, 146
**Flags,** 80, 128, 176, 224
**Florence, Italy,** 156, 170
**Folktale,** 76, 173
**Football,** 77
**France,** 147
**Fu Hao,** 118
**Fulani (Hausa/Fulani),** 75
**Fun with Social Studies,** 36–37, 84–85, 132–133, 180–181, 228–229
*Futebol,* 222

**Ganges River,** 99
**Garibaldi, Giuseppe,** 162, 163
**Generalize,** 104, 140–141, 145, 200

**Geographic features**
 archipelago, 99, *m99*
 basin, 195
 bay, 200
 bodies of water, 10
 climate, 12
 coastline, 147
 delta, 56, *m57*, 61
 desert, 49, 50, 51, 52, 98, 104, *m105*, 194, 195, 200
 elevation, 196
 fresh water, 10
 fjord, 142, 146
 forest, 49, 98, 194, 195
 glacier, 190, 194
 gulf, 10, 45, 56, 57
 hills, 9, 50, 57, 152
 island, 98, 99, 146, 152
 lake, 4–5, 10, 11, 49, 50, 57, 152, *m153*
 monsoon, 100
 mountain, 9, 49, 50, 52, *m57*, 97, 98, *m99*, 104, *m105*, 146, 152, *m153*, 193, 194, 195, 196, 200
 ocean, 10, 18, 56, 57, 97, 98, 99, *m99*, 104, 147, 195
 peninsula, 94, 99, *m99*, 146, 152
 plain, 9, 49, 50, 98, 146, 152, 194
 plateau, 9, 50, 57, 97, 98, *m99*, 104, *m105*
 rain forest 51, 52, 57, 98, 101, 193, 194, 200, 214–215
 river, 10, 11, 18, 45, 49, 50, 56, 57, *m57*, 99, *m99*, 104, *m105*, 147, *m153*, 193, 194, 195
 salt water, 10
 savanna, 51, 52, 57
 sea, 10, 99, 110, 147, 148, 152, *m153*
 steppe, 98, 101
 strait, 195
 tributary, 195
 tundra, 97, 98, 101
 valley, 11, 49, 50, 152, 153, *m153*
 waterfall, 49
 wetland, 57
**Geography,** 10
 Africa, 49–53
 Asia, 97–101
 Brazil, 200–201
 China, 104–105
 Europe, 145–149
 Italy, 152–153
 Nigeria, 56–57
 South America, 193–197

**Germany**

**Germany,** 147
**Gilberto, Astrud,** 220
**Glacier,** 190, 194
**Glossary,** *R24–R29*
**Gobi Desert,** 98, *m99*, 104
**Golden Law,** 210
**Golden Rule,** 130
**Gotel Mountains,** *m57*
**Government,** 7, 32
   Brazil, 212
   change, 33
   China, 116
   democracy, 32
   Italy, 160, 164
   Nigeria, 70
   United States, 33
**Grand Canal, Venice,** 158–159
**Graph and Image Analysis**
  **Skills,** 64, 70, 75, 116, 211, 212
  decoding images, 61, 71, 79, 109, 117, 127, 157, 165, 175, 205, 213, 223
  graphs, 43, 75, 91, 101–102, 103, 110, 139, 187
  paintings, 158–159
**Graph and Chart Skills,**
  Read a Bar Graph, 102–103
  Read a History Timeline, 64–65
**Great Britain,** 33, 68–69
**Great European Plain,** 146, *m147*
**Great Lakes,** 4–5
**Great Rift Valley,** 50, 51
**Great Wall of China,** 89, 113
**Greece,** 146
**Guanabara Bay, Brazil,** 200
**Guangzhou, China,** *m107*
**Gulf of Guinea,** 45, 56

**Han dynasty,** 119
**Hausa,** 67, 75
**Hemisphere,** 198
**Heritage,** 75
**Hieroglyphics,** 34–35
**High-tech,** 202, 206–207
**Himalayas,** 98, *m99*, 104
**Holidays**
  Chinese New Year, 129
  Christmas, 78
  Independence Day (Brazil), 225
  Liberation Day (Italy), 177
  Ramadan, 78
  Republic Day (Italy), 177
**Huang He,** 104

**Hudson River,** 18
**Human resources,** 17
**Hunter-gatherers,** 208
**Hydroelectric power,** 190, 201

**Ife, Nigeria,** *m58*, 67
**Igbo,** 66, 67, 75
**Iguaçu Falls,** *m201*
**Immigration,** 218
**Import,** 108, 153
**Independence,** 69, 201
**Independence Day, Brazil,** 225
**Indian Ocean,** 98, 99
**Indian Peninsula,** *m99*
**Indians, South American,** 193
  of Brazil, 208–209, 218
  Yanomami, 208
**Industry,** 46, 58, 106, 108, 154–158, 159, 202–203
**Infographics Features**
  High-Tech Brazil, 206–207
  Language Regions of the World, 26–27
  Made in China, 110–111
  Nigeria's Oil, 62–63
  Roman House, 166–167
**Italian Opera,** 172
**Intermediate directions,** 14
**Internet,** 91, 150
**Inventions, Chinese,** 113
**Irrigation,** 105
**Islam, in Nigeria,** 78
**Italy**
  Bargnani, Andrea, 179
  Belmondo, Stefania, 179
  bodies of water, 152
  Cannavaro, Fabio, 178
  celebrations and holidays, 176–177
  climate, 153
  Colosseum, 160, 161
  culture, 162, 170–174
  current issues and problems, 164
  economy, 152, 154
  flag, 176
  gondolas, *m155*, 158
  government, 160, 164
  history, 160–163
  holidays, 174, 177
  jobs in, *m154–155*
  land, 152
  landforms, 152, *m153*, 158
  location, 152

  people and groups, 163, 170, 173, 178–179
  population, 170
  products and industries, 154, *m154–155*
  regions, 153, 170
  resources, 153
  Sardinia, 152
  service jobs, 155
  seal, 176
  Sicily, 152, 156
  symbols, 176
  tourism in, 156
  volcano, 156

**Japan,** 99
**Japanese archipelago,** *m99*
**Jesus,** 78
**Jews, in Brazil,** 219
*Jingxi,* 124, 125
*Ju ju,* 77
**June Festivals,** 225

**Kalahari Desert,** 51
**Kano, Nigeria,** *m59*
**Kilimanjaro, Mount,** 49
**Korean Peninsula,** *m99*

**Lagos, Nigeria,** 45, *m58*, 60, 68
**Lake Baikal,** 11
**Lake Como,** 152
**Lake Erie,** 5
**Lake Huron,** 5
**Lake Malawi,** 51
**Lake Mead,** 11
**Lake Michigan,** 5
**Lake Ontario,** 5
**Lake Superior,** 5
**Lake Tanganyika,** 51
**Lake Victoria,** 50
**Landform,** 9, 49–50, 56–57, 97–99, 104–105, 146, 152, 193–194, 200, 214–215
**Language,** 22–23, 26–27, 74–75, 122, 170, 187
**Language Regions,** 26–27
**Lantern Festival,** 129
**Latitude,** 198, *m198*
**Leisure time,** 191, 222
**Liberation Day,** 177
**Limón, Costa Rica,** 18

Lisboa, Antônio Francisco, 220
Literature, 173, 220
London, England, 147
Longitude, 198, *m198*
Look Closely at Primary
  Sources
  Egyptian Hieroglyphics, 34–35
  Royal Art of Benin, 72–73
  Sayings of Confucius, 130–131
  Venice's Grand Canal, 158–
    159
  Visiting the Amazon Rain
    Forest, 214–215

Machu Picchu, 185
Main Idea and Details, 4–5, 9,
  22, 74, 122, 160, 218
Malay Peninsula, *m99*
Manicoré, Brazil, 202
Manufacturing, 58
  Brazil, 202–203
  China, 106–108
  Italy, 154–155
  Nigeria, 58–59
Mao Zedong, 115, 116
Map and Globe Skills
  Reading maps, legends,
    symbols, and scales, 14–15,
    54–55
  Using a compass rose, grids,
    and time zones, 198–199
Map key, 14
Map scale, 54
Maps
  Africa: Physical, *mR13*
  Africa: Political, *mR12*
  Africa Today, *m42*
  Asia: Physical, *mR16–17*
  Asia: Political, *mR14–R15*
  Asia Today, *m90–91*
  Asia's Landforms, *m99*
  Brazil, Jobs in, *m202–203*
  Brazil's Landforms, *m201*
  China, Jobs in, *m106–107*
  China's Landforms, *m105*
  Cities in Africa, *m55*
  Europe: Physical, *mR20–21*
  Europe: Political, *mR18–R19*
  Europe Today, *m138–139*
  Europe's Landforms, *m147*
  Italy, Jobs in, *m154–155*
  Italy's Landforms, *m153*
  Language Regions of the
    World, *m26–27*
  New York, *m39*
  Nigeria, Jobs in, *m58–59*

  Nigeria, Kingdoms in Early,
    *m67*
  Nigeria's Landforms, *m57*
  Physical Features of Africa,
    *m51*
  Roman Empire, *m161*
  South America: Physical, *mR23*
  South America: Political, *mR22*
  South America Today, *m186–
    187*
  South America's Landforms,
    *m195*
  United States: Physical, *mR10–
    R11*
  United States: Political, *mR8–
    R9*
  World, *m2–3, m15, m199*
  World: Physical, *mR6–R7*
  World: Political, *mR4–R5*
Map title, 14
Market economy, 154
Martial art, 124, 125, 221
Mediterranean Sea, 50, 148
Mello, Fernando Collor de, 211
Milan, Italy, 154
Millennium, 64
Mining, 107
Moderate, 148
Modernize, 191, 210
Monarchy, 210
Monsoon, 100
Muslim, 78
Mount Etna, 156
Mount Everest, *m99*
Mount Pinatubo, 93
Muhammad, 78
Mumbai, India, 97
Muir, John, 20
Music
  Astrud Gilberto, 220
  Bossa nova, 220
  Brazilian Popular Music, 220
  Italian Opera, 173
  *jingxi*, 124, 125
  *ju ju*, 77
  King Sunny Ade, 77
  Nigeria, 76, 77
Muslims, in Nigeria, 78

Namib Desert, 51
Naples, Italy, *m155*
Natural resources, 6, 16
  coal, 57, 105, 149, 153, 197
  cobalt, 53
  columbite, 57
  conservation of, 19, 20–21
  copper, 53, 100, 106, 197

  diamonds, 53
  fish, 57, 149, 153, 197
  forests, 53, 57, 100, 149, 197,
    201
  gold, 53, 100, 197
  iron ore, 53, 57, 100, 105, 106,
    149
  minerals, 53, 57, 100, 149, 201
  natural gas, 153
  oil, 53, 57, 100, 153, 197
  recycling, 19
  reusing, 19
  silver, 100
  soil, 53, 57, 100, 105, 149,
    153, 201
  tin, 57, 197
  water, 100, 105, 149, 153
Needs, 24
Netherlands, 147
New York
  state map of, *m39*
New York City
  Hudson River, 18
  resources of, 18
  Unisphere, 1
Niger River, 50, 56
Nigeria
  Abuja, 70
  Ade, King Sunny, 77
  Benin, Kingdom of, 67, *m67*,
    72–73
  bodies of water, 56, 57, 58
  celebrations and holidays, 78,
    80–81
  climate, 57
  colony, 68
  culture, 74, 75, 76, 82
  current issues and problems,
    60
  Edo, Kingdom of, 67
  early kingdoms, 66–67
  economy, 56, 58
  flag, 80
  geography, 56–57
  government, 66, 69, 70
  Gulf of Guinea, 56, 57
  Hausa, 67
  history, 66–69
  Ife, 67
  Igbo, 66–67
  jobs in, *m58–59*
  *ju ju*, 77
  Kingdoms in early, *m67*
  land, 56
  landforms, 56–61, *m57*
  location, 56
  Nok, 66
  Obasanjo, Olusegun, 69
  oil, 62–63
  Oyo, Kingdom of, 67

Nile River

people and groups, 66–67, 72–75, 82
political map of, *m59*
Port Harcourt, 59
products and industries, 58, *m58–59*
religion, 78
resources, 57, 59, 62–63
seal, 80
slavery in, 68
soccer, 43, 77
Soyinka, Wole, 82–83
Super Falcons, 77
symbols, 80
vegetation, 57, 59
wildlife, 57, 59
Yoruba, 67
**Nile River,** 11, 49, 50
**Nok,** 66
**Norway,** 24, 146

**Oba,** 72–73
**Obasanjo, Olusegun,** 69
**Oil,** 57, 58, 59, 62–63, 100
**Opera, Italian,** 172
**Orange, France,** 141
**Orinoco River,** 195, 208
**Osun Oshogbo,** 81
**Oyo, Nigeria,** 67

**Pacific Ocean,** 98, 99, 195
**Painting,** 162, 173, 221
**Palermo, Italy,** *m155*
**Pampas,** 194, *m195*
**Panama Canal,** 195
**Pantheon, Rome,** 141
**Paraguay-Paraná River,** 195
**Pedro I,** 210
**Pedro II,** 210
**Peninsula,** 94, 99, 146
**Petroleum,** 57, 58, 62–63, 100.
*See also* Oil.
**Pinocchio,** 173
**Po River Valley, Italy,** 152, 153
**Point of view,** 216
**Pollution,** 106
**Popular music,** Brazilian, 221
**Population,** 170
Africa, 43
Asia, 91, 97
Brazil, 218
China, 104, 122
Europe, 43, 139
Italy, 170

Nigeria, 66–67
South America, 187
**Port Harcourt, Nigeria,** *m59*
**Portugal,** 209
**Potomac River,** 45
**Primary source,** 120
**Primary Sources, Look Closely**
Confucian Sayings, 130–131
Egyptian Hieroglyphics, 34–35
Royal Art of Benin, 72–73
Venice's Grand Canal, 158–159
Visiting the Amazon Rain Forest, 214–215
**Prime Meridian,** 198, *mR6–R7*
**Problem and Solution,** 152
**Producer,** 154
**Projects**
bulletin board, 184
class magazine, 136
culture fair, 232
nature center exhibit, 40
resource booklet, 88
**Protestants, in Brazil,** 219
**Pyramids,** 30
**Pyrenees,** 146

**Qin dynasty,** 112
**Qing dynasty,** 114

**Rain forest,** 51, 52, 57, 98, 101, 193, 194, 200, 214–215
**Ramadan,** 78
**Reading Maps,** 51, 57, 59, 99, 105, 106, 153, 154, 195, 201, 202, 203
**Reading Skills**
Categorize, 16
Cause and Effect, 56, 193
Compare and Contrast, 49
Generalize, 104, 145, 200
Main Idea and Details, 9, 22, 74, 122, 160, 218
Problem and Solution, 152
Sequence, 28, 66, 112, 208
Summarize, 97, 170
**Reading Social Studies Skills**
Cause and Effect, 188–189
Compare and Contrast, 44–45
Generalize, 140–141
Main Idea and Details, 4–5
Summarize, 92–93
**Red Sea,** 50
**Reference book,** 150

**Region,** 18
Africa, 50
Asia, 98–100, *m99*
Brazil, 200, 204
China, 105
Europe, 148, 152
Italy, 153, 170
Nigeria, 56
South America, 193, 196
**Religions,** 23
of Brazil, 219
Buddhism, 219
Candomblé, 219
Catholicism, 170, 219
Christianity, 78
Islam, 78, 80
Judaism, 219
of Nigeria, 78, 80
Protestantism, 162
**Renaissance,** 162
**Republic,** 114, 160, 163, 211
**Republic Day,** 177
**Research and Writing Skills**
Getting information,150–151
Interpreting information, 34–35, 72–73, 120–121, 130–131, 158–159, 214–215
**Resources**
capital, 17
human, 17
natural, 16
**Respect for ancestors,** 123
**Rhine River,** 147
**Ring of Fire,** 93
**Rio de Janeiro, Brazil,** 200, 203, 204, 211
**Roman Catholic Church,** 170, 219
**Roman Empire,** 161, *m161*
**Roman Republic,** 160, 161
**Rome,** *m155*, 156, 160, 161, 172
**Royal Art of Benin,** 72
**Rubber,** 202
**Rural,** 60
Brazil, 204, 219
China, 123, 126
Italy, 171
Nigeria, 60
**Russia,** 97

**Sahara,** 49, 51
**São Paulo, Brazil,** 203, 204
**Sardinia,** 152
**Savanna,** 51, 52
**School**
Brazil, 222
China, 126